THE FOUNDATIONS OF ISLAMIC ECONOMICS AND BANKING

THE FOUNDATIONS OF ISLAMIC ECONOMICS AND BANKING

Abdulrahman Haitham Shoukat Kabbara

PARTRIDGE

A Penguin Random House Company

To order additional copies of this book, contact
Toll Free 800 101 2657 (Singapore)
Toll Free 1 800 81 7340 (Malaysia)
orders.singapore@partridgepublishing.com

www.partridgepublishing.com/singapore

CONTENTS

PART II
THE ISLAMIC ALTERNATIVE

PART III
THE IMPACT OF A RIBA-FREE ECONOMY

Dedicated to my parents and my family

About the Author

Abdulrahman Haitham S. Kabbara earned his PhD from Loughborough University of Technology-UK after receiving BA and MBA from Damascus University and Hartford University-USA respectively. His PhD thesis demonstrates the possibility of transforming an interest-based finanancial system in Kuwait into an interest-free one by applying appropriate strategies and policies. He is currently providing consulting services to the Kuwait Foundation for the Advancement of Sciences. He served as Financial-Shari'a Advisor to The International Investor and coordinator for the Shari' a Board. In his capacity as Senior Economist with Hill-SDPM, consultant of mega project in Kuwait, He conducted projects' evaluation, proposed privatization ventures, steered PPP and BOT projects. He is the founder and chairman of Future Consultations establishment and the Lebanese Investment Company (invest), the first interest-free shareholding company in Lebanon. He also was Executive Vice President at Attamar Economic Consultations in Kuwait. During his tenure at the Industrial bank in Kuwait, he was awarded a stipend to obtain a Doctorate degree. He was entrusted by IBK Chairman to promote industrial projects on interest-free basis in cooperation with the Kuwait Finance House. He teaches courses in engineering economics, managerial finance and Islamic banking and economics. He conducted training programs in monetary policy at the Institute of Banking Studies in Kuwait. His primary areas of interest are evaluation for merger and acquisitions, auditing and reviewing products in compliance with Shari'a principles, essay writing and research. He contributed to solving the debt crisis in Kuwait based on Islamic principles.

Foreword

By
Adnan Al-Bahar
Chairman and Managing Director of
The International Investor, Kuwait

The book starts with an illuminating introduction to Islamic economics and finance that attempts to explain the foundations of economics from an Islamic perspective. The author discusses the structures as well as the theoretical and practical aspects of the Islamic economic ideology with clarity and insight. He also provides a comprehensive overview of some of the main topics still under scrutiny, such as the link between private and public ownership and the role of money.

Islamic finance is an important supplement to the financial intermediation infrastructure of any country, but especially those with a large Muslim population. Without it, that infrastructure cannot operate optimally. Islamic finance, when applied sincerely and in line with the spirit and intent of Sharia, can help alleviate some of the financial problems facing companies in today's global market crisis. The industry, however, still has much ground to cover, especially in capital market products, including securitization and sukuk, subordinated debt, and Mudaraba funding.

This book accomplishes the following:

- It simultaneously serves as a practical reference for Islamic economics and finance.
- It provides a new spirit of innovation, socially responsible discipline, and new financial tools to countries with a financial intermediation infrastructure and a large Muslim population.
- It compares conventional with Islamic economic principles.

- It assesses the efficiency of an Islamic financial system at the macro and micro levels.
- It focuses on Islamic economics from a global perspective.

This book is a sincere effort to expound upon the features of Islamic finance for anyone who wants to probe more deeply into this industry's continued development.

Adnan Al Bahar
Kuwait

21/6/1433h-May 1, 2012

Preface

The Foundations of Islamic Economics and Banking
by Dr. A. Haitham Shoukat Kabbara

My interest in riba-free banking dates back many years. My father, a merchant and owxner of ready-made clothing, was like any businessman, mainly worried about fund raising and liquidity shortages. Seldom did he deal with banks and, when he did, it was merely to cash a check or to pay for imported goods. When he needed cash for working capital, he borrowed from friends or relatives or engaged with them in partnership on profit and loss sharing schemes.

I used to spend most summer mornings at my father's workshop and the afternoons as a sales person in his retail shop. When I turned 15, I began to argue with my father about his motives for not borrowing from banks. "Interest is haram (forbidden), and riba is unlawful . . . ," he used to tell me, God bless his soul. "But interest is not riba," I would say. His dialog with me was always firm and decisive, explaining the harm riba causes, the blessings associated with profit sharing, the rewards awarded to buyers and sellers, and the punishments awaiting the nonbelievers.

Uttering the Holy verse, "Sale is like riba and God has permitted sale and forbidden riba . . ." (surat al-Baqara) Despite my deep devotion and pure conviction in God's teachings, I always felt something was missing, an alternative system. In 1962, I decided to transfer from medical school to economics school before the first year of university. My motives were more than justified on the grounds that *"abolishing riba (or usury) and the reorganization of banks,* as I wrote in my diary, *was a worthy goal to pursue,"* even more satisfying than walking the paths ploughed in Africa by Dr. Schweitzer, whose sacrifices inspired so many youth at the time.

The leap between abolishing riba and restructuring the banking system does not seem so unattainable. We need to narrow the gap between our beliefs and our practices. Courage is needed and a well-planned alternative is within our reach. This book is part of my thesis which was submitted for partial fulfillment of the requirements for the award of Doctor of Philosophy in 1988 at Loughborough University of Technology.[1] Its theme hovers on the ways and means to convert the conventional banking system into Islamic principles, emphasizing the case of Kuwait. Certain alterations and modifications were made to the thesis to produce the current book. While the basic structure of Part I remains intact, it now stresses the origins of Islamic economic thinking, outlining the basic features of Islamic economics. Parts II and III cover an Islamic alternative, introducing new subjects and updating earlier ones, particularly types of financing operations. Part III has been reorganized, emphasizing the economic impact and efficiency of a riba-free system over the conventional one.

---

[1]   Abdulrahman Haitham S. Kabbara, "Islamic Banking, a Case Study of Kuwait," Loughborough University of Technology, Loughborough, unpublished PhD thesis, December 1988.

Acknowledgments

I would like to thank Mr. Anwar Al-Nouri who as chairman of the Industrial Bank at the time has financed the major part of my research. Special gratitude is due to His Excellency Sheikh Khaled Aljarrah who manifests the true spirit of Islamic financial dealings.

Am particularly indebted to my colleague Dr. Anas al Zarqa for his suggestions and valuable insight, which were helpful at all stages of writing and revision. I am also grateful to Dr. Abd Assatar Abu Ghudeh, Peter Sadler, John Presley, Khurshid Ahmed, M. Mannan, Dr. M. N. Siddiqi, Jaafer Abbas and Dr. Rafic Al-Masri for their illuminating discussions and encouragement. My thanks goes also to Adnan Al-Bahar and Abdulwahab Al-Tammar.

Credits are due to the editors, especially Dr. Badwi Al Shahal, Trafford Associates for their efforts to ensure a quality product.

Many thanks go to Shibu Eappens, Ghazwa, Bassel, Fayzah Dima, and Dunia Kabbara for their typing assistance.

Looking forward to the implementation of a riba-free economy in Kuwait and all Islamic countries, I sincerely hope this book will contribute toward this historic God-blessed achievement.

Kuwait, March 14, 2012
A.Haitham S.Kabbara

CHAPTER 1

Introduction

In the aftermath of the Islamic resurgence movement, the call for the abolition of interest and the introduction of profit and loss sharing schemes has gained momentum. The first riba-free savings bank was initiated by the late Dr. Ahmad Alnajjar in 1963 in Mit Ghamr, Egypt. The bank's depositors were mainly farmers who received financing to purchase raw materials and simple equipment. The financing mode was either musharaka-that is, on a profit and loss sharing basis, or qard hasan (benevolent loan). This experiment survived until 1967. Several factors attributed to its decline, such as a narrow deposit base, a liquidity shortage, a lack of professional bank employee training, few industrial and trading opportunities, and the absence of an entity that could act as the bank's last resort.

Today, almost 40 years since the Mit Ghamr experiment, the economic transformation from a conventional to a riba-free economy has apparently slowed, if not stagnated entirely. Only three Islamic countries-the Sudan, Iran, and Pakistan-claim to apply riba-free principles in their local banking transactions. Shari'a sources, however, deny that these countries have transformed their entire banking structure into a riba-free system. Although this book does not aim to evaluate the movement from conventional to Islamic finance principles, some discussion of that process is necessary.

The dilemma the Islamic world is facing is the wide gap between Shari'a principles and practice. Presently the actions of both the rulers and the ruled are far from—if not in contradiction to—ordained instructions. More than one explanation for this state of affairs exists, including weak beliefs and convictions, conflict between reason and faith, and the rise and fall of the nation of Islam. This state of affairs has contributed greatly to widening the gap between Shari'a theory and practice as well as to the confusion and subtle identity of the Muslim world. The uninterrupted decline and upsurge of the nation of Islam deserve few comments:

The Messenger of God ruled in Almadina only for 11 years (01h-11). Al Khulafa'ur-Rashideen ("rightly guided successors") to the messenger of God ruled 30 years (632-661). They were pretty much occupied by consolidating the Islamic rule. In the wake of continued threat from neighboring infidels and enemies of Islam, the emerging state was obliged for the sake of security and survival to expand in the East to Persia, in the North to Syria and in the West to Egypt. The Omayyad dynasty that succeeded the Khulafa'ur-Rashideen in Damascus lasted 90 years (661-750) and faced several uprising. Followed by the Abbasid (750-1258) who encouraged culture, science and built an irrigation system which was unique in their times. Caliph alMansur built Baghdad, the crown jewel of the Abbasid, in 762. Established by Caliph Harun al-Rashid in the ninth century, *Beit ul Hikmah* was a library and translation institute, an unrivaled center for the study of the humanities and sciences, including mathematics, medicine, alchemy, astronomy, zoology, geography, and cartography. The weakening of the Abbasid khilafah mushroomed several dynasties. The Omayyad rule underwent a revival in Andalusia, Spain, from 711. The Shiite Fatimid was able to establish its own dynasty (909-1171) in Tunisia and Egypt. Ultimately Islamic Khilafah broke down in the face of the Mongolian invasion of Baghdad in 1258. The demolition of Baghdad was a direct blow to the Islamic civilization. (*Beit ul Hikmah*) was destroyed and hundreds of thousands of books burned and thrown into the Tigress River as the troops crossed into the city. The liberation of Beit al-MaqdIs (Jerusalem) in 1187h by al-Zaher Salahuddin (Saladin) and the conquest of Constantinople (1458) paved the way to a revival of the Islamic golden age which flourished once again under the Ottoman Empire.

By the end of the First World War, Sultan Abdul-hamid II was topped down by Kamal Ataturk who declared Turkey a liberal state. Ever since the Islamic khilafa dissipated and never been revived up till now.

However, It is worthy of note that the first Shari'a-based contractual civil code was written during the Ottoman regime and Ottoman law is among the main sources of many Muslim nations' civil code.

In addressing the gap between Shari'a principles and real practice various components must be examined: the contractual, the financial, and the commercial.

At the contractual level, a conflict subsists between predominantly civil laws and the Ottoman code. Since the 18th century new instruments and types of contracts have emerged in the West and have been adopted by Muslim countries. Moreover, the diversity of Muslims schools of thought precludes any attempt for unified codes unless an authoritative body decides on the appropriate school to be adopted. Such an entity does not exist and may not for many years to come; it is difficult to positively address these issues within the Arab and Islamic countries.

The majority of the Arab countries, including the three mentioned earlier, have a dual financial and banking system: one Islamic and the second conventional. How long this duplication will last is anybody's guess. Although many public and private organizations and institutions within the Islamic world actively support and supervise research aimed at simplifying, explaining, or bridging the gap between Shari'a and the contemporary world, the State of Kuwait has been alone in taking methodical and practical steps. The late Emir of Kuwait Sheikh Jaber al-Ahmed issued a decree establishing the Higher Committee for the Transformation of Shari'a. This committee has since been engaged in laying the groundwork for a smooth transformation process.

At the commercial level, this book describes the interaction between the origins and ideology of Shari'a principles and commercial transactions. The origins of Islamic jurisprudence are manifested in the Quran, the Prophet's habitual practice, and jurists' interpretations. This book focuses on teachings that originated during the mid-sixth century (AD), relating to commercial transactions. These teachings treasures still are and will forever remain a milestone in commercial and financial contractual relationships and economic development.

The prohibition of riba does not mean that profit and loss sharing is the only method available in the market. The prohibition of riba is not intended to thwart business or put an end to thriving trade and financial activities in the Moslem world, for "God has permitted trade" (*Surat al-Baqara*) and the Shari'a has laid down a respective code of economic activities. The code's driving theme is freedom in transactions rather than prohibition. It forbids transactions, for instance, only to preclude cheating, deceiving, fraud, theft, (gharar) or undue influence by the stronger party in a contract over the weaker. However, the gap between Islamic principles and merchants' behavior is not expected to narrow in the short run.

At the financial level, the prohibition of riba and interest has paved the way for the establishment of riba-free financial institutions. A development of this magnitude is only possible because contemporary Islamic economists and jurists have established a framework for the theoretical and organizational structure of an Islamic economy. Although

More than 1.4 billion people throughout the world believe in the origins of Islamic jurisprudence and its distinctive teachings and directives. Unfortunately this conviction is not accompanied by rightful applications. Many factors contribute to this phenomenon and have played a part in violating Islamic principles in commercial transactions, including Ignorance, illiteracy, a lack of Shari'a education, greed, and immoral practices.

Most of the Muslim world consists of developing nations. The majority of the 57 members of the Organization of Islamic Countries (OIC) are poor in natural resources (except agricultural land) and skilled manpower. Most of their citizens live below the poverty line and suffer from illiteracy; nearly one in three people in the Arab world is illiterate (2010)[1]. The Arab world also suffers from the highest percentage of unemployment, exceeding 10.3% compared with 6.2% globally[2].

At the same time, a few Arab states are among the richest in the world in per capita income due to oil and cash surplus and reserves. The difference in income between the richest and poorest Islamic countries is of the order of 220 times.

The contribution of the wealthy Islamic countries to the poor and developing nations generally as a percentage of their gross domestic product surpasses 7.5%, far exceeding the 1-2% of the United States. In contrast, the total production of the 57 Islamic countries does not exceed that of Germany and Japan combined.[3] In addition, their contribution to scientific research is the lowest, not exceeding $1.7 billion, or 0.2% of their gross domestic product[4], compared to 2.7% for France, 3% for Japan and 4.7% for Israel. In contrast, the total value of video sales in the Arab world is $16 billion and Arab women spend $2 billion per year on cosmetics, with a total annual income of $35 billion earned by Asian maids working in Arab countries.

On top of that, the fifty seven members of the OIC states have only 500 universities compared with 5000 in the USA and 8000 in India.

The demand for Shari'a compliant services and financial products is increasing by 15% per year. Furthermore, according to Kuala Lumpur-based international financial services, Shari'a trade finance may reach $800 billion this year. Trade among members of the OIC is relatively weak not exceeding 15% currently compared with their world wide trade volume. According to the Accounting and Auditing Organizations for Islamic Financial Institutions (AAOIFI), trade among the OIC members will reach only around $5 trillion to $6 trillion in 2015.

The Islamic and the Arab world are facing a dilemma on the political, social and economic levels despite the fact that Islamic banks' assets will rise to $16 trillion by 2012. Unfortunately 50% of all Arab and Islamic countries' bank balance sheets are in the form of idle cash balance. This may partially explain why unemployment has not been the only linchpin factor behind the recent uprisings in all Arab and Islamic countries. Recall the slogans raised by youth particularly in many of these countries appealing for jobs, freedom, justice, equality, political reforms, sustainable development and redistribution of wealth.

Some Islamic countries had experimented with capitalism, others with socialism. However, none of these theories has offered a solution to the problems of illiteracy, poverty and unemployment. Does this mean that we should seek a third path to follow? Is this path an Islamic oriented theory such as the Islamic economy? In fact the problem is more complicated and diverse in scope and magnitude. This book is but an initial attempt towards answering few queers pertaining to the right path to follow provided certain conditions prevail. Hopefully a compilation of further researches and advanced studies would contribute to formulating a sustainable economic theory.

Book Organization

Researchers have examined Islamic banking operations in an interest-based economy and outlined the Islamic economy's principles and functions, there has not yet been a comprehensive study dealing with the implications of abolishing interest in an Islamic economy or any specific country.

In exploring the possibility of abolishing interest, this book analyzes the interface between Islam and economics to detail the underlying theory. It adopts an analytical and pragmatic approach. The economic factors embedded in its study do not lend themselves to economic modeling because there are too many variables and many solutions to the same problem. I wish to point out, however, that my analysis is not purely academic but embraces practical implications and suggests many paths in the implementation of an Islamic economy or the transfer from a conventional economy to an Islamic one.

This book is organized into three parts. Part I presents the origins of Islamic economic thinking and its underlying principles. The Islamic views concerning wealth and ownership, labor, social justice, money and Riba were examined. Such an understanding is the cornerstone for any transformation from a conventional economic system to a new Islamic paradigm.

Part II describes the Islamic alternative pertaining to riba-free banking theory and the prospects of implementing the new system. It analyzes Islamic and Western theories, comparing the two systems by focusing on riba-free financing techniques and the operation of money and capital markets. This section also looks at the implications of riba-free banking with reference to Kuwait and the pros and cons of this experiment.

Part III analyzes the impact of a riba-free economy at the macro and micro levels, examining the efficiency of the Islamic financial system with respect to competition and choice, aggregate savings and investments, earning stability, fund pricing, savings mobilization, financial instruments, risk attached to traditional forms of Islamic finance, and, finally, the impact of zakat on savings and investments. The advantages and disadvantages of riba-free banking in the economy are also analyzed.

The final chapter summarizes the book's findings and recommendations.

Hope this work will contribute to the current debate on Islamic banking in general and comparative economics in particular.

Abdulrahman Haitham S. Kabbara
Kuwait, January 25, 2012

Endnotes:

1. According to Tunis-based Arab League Education, Culture and Scientific Organization (Alecso).
2. International Labor Organization (ILO).
3. Rifat Oglo, Investment Conference, Islamic Chamber of Commerce and Industry (ICCI), Amman, Jordan, May 22 25, 2011.
4. Hussain Haggani, Reasons for decline of the Muslim world. Gulf News, May 2, 2007

PART I

ORIGINS of ISLAMIC ECONOMICS

Chapters 2 to 7 outline the Islamic origins of economic thinking and its analyzing the economic implications of Islam by focusing on the economic concepts of the Quran and all economic oriented teachings that Islam has substantially addressed such as:

Wealth and ownership in Islam.
Work and productivity.
The Islamic state and economic intervention.
The distribution system and social justice.
Demand for money in the Islamic economy.
Riba in the Islamic jurisprudence.

Other concepts with modern implications, such as money and capital markets, as well as the macro and microeconomic implications of an interest free economy are also discussed.

CHAPTER 2

Islamic Economic Thinking

I n addition to religious teachings, Islam governs the moral, socio economic and political affairs of a society. It follows that Islamic economics are mainly based upon the Islamic value system. This link between Islamic values and economics can be inferred from the rules and injunctions incorporated of Shari'a, or Islamic law. The word *Shari'a* literally means path or guide it describes the path to virtue. This chapter discusses the sources of Islamic law followed by an outline of the philosophical aspects as well as characteristics and principles of the Islamic economic system. It will also examine issues such as normative and positive economics, ethics and economics, and economic problems.

This book describes the principal foundations of Islamic economics from Islamic teachings embedded in Islamic law, or *fiqh*. By scrutinizing Shari'a doctrine, economists can explain macro matters such as the basic structure of an interest-free economy and subjects closely associated with the tools and mechanism of an Islamic economy: for example, all legal aspects of the prohibition of interest, rules pertaining to moral teachings such as opposition to fraud and corruption and regulations pertaining to commercial transactions in the markets through *hisba* (supervision of markets) and the *beit al-mal* (the Treasury), including revenues and taxation. This book also investigates the rules of *zakat* (alms tax), *waqf* (charitable trust), and, last but not least, price fixing and expropriation in the public interest.

The Origins of Islamic Economic Thinking

Islam is an ideology comprising a set of principles and doctrines that guide and regulate a Muslim's relations with God and society. These doctrines are characterized by the notion that Islam is not only a divine service (such as Judaism or Christianity) but also involves all aspects of life. The Islamic code of conduct regulates and organizes the immediate concerns and activities of mankind in their spiritual and material life. Thus the code of worldly conduct is the divine law that guides Muslims in their economic, political, social, and cultural affairs. In contrast, the economics of capitalism are a secular or man-made law.

The principles of Islamic economic theory are basically found in legally binding precedents known to be the sources of Islamic jurisprudence (*usul al fiqh*)[1], in the following order.

Quran:	The book of revelations made to Prophet Mohammad (*saas*) by God
Almighty. *Hadith*:	Quoted conversations relating the Prophet's deeds and utterances.
Sunna:	The Prophet Mohammad's habitual practices and behavior
Ijma':	Consensus reached after intensive deliberations (consultations) among religious scholars on points or issues facing the nation and not envisaged in the *Quran* or *Sunna*.
Qiyas:	Deduction by analogy, as in giving an opinion on a case (not referred to in the *Quran* or *Sunna*) in comparison with another case referred to in the *Quran* or *Sunna*. This is accomplished by virtue of the similarity in the causes for decree (ordinance) between the two cases.
Ijtihad:	Jurists' independent reasoning (by deduction) relating to the applicability of certain Shari'a rules on each and every case not mentioned in the *Quran* or *Sunna*. Independent reasoning was terminated in the fourth century of the *Hijra*[2].

Certain judicial theologians consider other norms emanating from the original sources, called *furuh*, which involve *istihsan* (habitual preference) and *istislah* (social utility). *Istihsan* relates to new judgments and guidelines reflecting changes in customs in non-religious matters; every Shari'a principle based on customs (*urf*) can be altered when these customs are changed. *Istislah* is a flexible device based on opinions drawn from experience, provided they do not violate Shari'a principles.

The Sunni majority follows four schools of thought (*Madhaheb, sing. Madhhab*) in Islamic law: the Hanafi, the Shafi'i, the Maliki, and the Hanbali Schools. These schools represent the Sunni Muslims. There is also the Ja'afari School, which represents the Shiite minority. In all schools, the Quran and Sunna are the original sources of Shari'a.

These schools, however, use different methods in *qiyas*: Their interpretation and deduction may vary, for example, with respect to a word in the original sources that has multiple meanings or when an authentic hadith is transmitted to one school of thought and not to the others.[3]

Sunna, sometimes referred to as *jomhour* (majority), accepts all sayings of the Prophet, irrespective of the narrator, provided the narrator is trustworthy. Of the four schools of the Sunna, the Hanafis rely the most heavily on *qiyas* and *istihsan* (social utility. The Shafi'is acknowledge the superiority of *ijma'* over a hadith transmitted by only one person or unconfirmed by other transmitters. They also permit *istishab,* calling it *al-munasebeh* (convenience). For the Malikis, the authentic *ahadith* (plural of *hadith*) narrated by the Prophet's companions (*Sahaba*) supersede qiyas. A genuine hadith attributed to a single narrator ranks higher than one attributed to many, provided the former is in compliance with the customs and traditions of the inhabitants of Al-Madina or Hijaz (provinces where the Prophet and his companions lived). The Hanbalis' deduction is very similar to that of the Shafi'is', except that authentic hadith, in their view, is superior to *qiyas, ijma',* or the Sahaba's own interpretations. The Shiite Muslims will not accept a hadith unless it was narrated by the Prophet's immediate family (particularly Caliph Ali and his descendants).

Deeds judged by these schools or Islamic Law in general fall into five categories:

1) prohibited (*haram*), 2) reprehensible (*makruh*),
3) indifferent (*mubah*), 4) meritorious (*mustabah*), and
5) obligatory (*wajib*).

Virtually all Islamic schools of thought agree that Shari'a rules aim to pursue the public good and avoid corruption. To fulfill these objectives, Islamic law aims at preserving five instinctive necessities:

1. *Al-Deen* (religion).
2. *Al-Naf'es* (human being).

3. *Al-Aq'el* (mind).
4. *Al-Nas'el* (offspring).
5. *Al-Mal* (wealth).

When in doubt about an injunction or ruling, a Muslim relates the case to one or more of these fulcrums. Accordingly, Al-Deen is superior to Al-Naf'es and preserving Al-Naf'es is superior to preserving Al-Mal.

Since this book is about Islamic economics not Islamic law, it is interesting to quote the Quran, a few Ahadith, and some of the rules of fiqh that guide the jurists in their ruling on worship as well as commercial matters:

Some fiqh rules[4]:

1. "Men shall have the benefit of what they earn, and women shall have the benefit of what they earn" (4:43).
2. "Only a sinful one hoards," narrated by Muslim, Ahmed, and Abu Dawoud.
3. "The burden is in proportion to the benefit and the benefit to the burden," related by Aisha.
4. "Delay by a solvent person is sin and may be punished as crime," Hadith Abu Hureira, narrated by al Bukhari wa Muslim.
5. "Liability is an obligation accompanying gain."
6. "Anything that serves as a means to the unlawful is also unlawful."
7. "Freedom of action in the field of mundane transactions is the rule."
8. "The Muslims are bound by their terms (*Shurutihin*)."
9. "Necessities make forbidden things allowed."
10. "A price is increased if it is deferred."

Are Islamic Economics Positive or Normative?

Islamic economics have been criticized for being normative describing what ought to be done as opposed to positive describing the facts as they are). Undeniably, Islamic economics are bound to remain substantially normative, particularly in its early phases of evolution, due to a tendency among Islamic economists to assume that economic agents behave categorically in line with Islamic economic precepts (and often make subjective statements moving between pure economics and political economy). For example, Hasanuzzaman defines Islamic economics as[5]:

> [The knowledge and application of injunctions and rules of the Shari'a that prevent injustice in the acquisition and disposal of material resources in order to provide satisfaction to human beings and enable them to perform their obligations to Allah and the Society].

This definition apparently ignores human behavior and its role in the economic process.

Baqr Al-Sadr believes that Islamic economics form a political economy as long as "we assume a certain social and economic paradigm based on certain foundations, and then we explain this assumed paradigm and explore its general characteristics in light of this foundation."[6] However, according to Al-Sadr, interpretations of many contemporary Islamic writers do not accurately represent the comprehensive scientific understanding of economic life in Islamic society, unless they depend on data obtained from real-world experience. There are usually contradictions between the real aspects of the system and explanations given on an assumed basis. When capitalist economists built their analytical theories on an assumed basis, they reached conclusions in contradiction with real life.

Ahmed attributes a global objective to Islamic economics by stating that "Islamic economics aims at the study of human *falah* achieved by organizing the resources of the Earth on the basis of co-operation and participation."[7] *Human falah*, is a vague term and could mean success or progress. Additionally, in Islam *falah* consists of spiritual and material elements that cannot be easily identified without subjective judgments.

I believe Islamic economists are far away from assigning global objectives for Islamic economics. At the outset they must try to apply fundamental economic principles that do not contradict with Shari'a. In any case a political economy must not be confused with pure economy. Furthermore, it is premature to address an international objective for Islamic economics in a diversified environment and wide dispersion of income, level of education and natural resources among each of the 57 Islamic states. The fact that Islamic economics are not applied anywhere in modern history precludes combining economic prediction with empirical testing, as is possible with positive economics. This has created a vacuum between prediction and hypothesis, on the one hand, and the real world on the other. Concurrently, generalization in Islamic economics has become quite difficult. Islamic economics, however, do not ignore the conventional tools of economic analysis such as elasticity, multipliers, and input/output analysis. The difference between the Islamic and conventional systems is that the first uses debatable data (i.e., hypothetical) in the analysis (up till now) while the second uses tangible data in the majority of cases.

Positive Economics, a Western View

Marshall (1824-1942) was the first among the neo classical school to hold the view that economics could be a science just like the natural sciences, but he took a broad approach to social science in which economics plays an important but limited role.

He recognized that in the real world, economic life is tightly bound up with ethical, social and political currents[8]. In his Essay on the Nature and Significance of Economic Science Robbins (1898-1984) redefined the scope of economics to be "the science which studies human behavior as a relationship between ends and scarce means which have alternative uses"[9]. Robbins, among others held the view that economics should be making scientific predictions and purely descriptive statements in order to be positive.[10]

Heilbroner, on the other hand, criticized the notion of scientific economics and stressed that even the so-called economic laws are built on subjective judgments, citing the example ofmaximization, which is based on value judgment and premises such as the belief that a higher growth rate is better than a lower one. The author then points out that a higher growth rate is not better if it leads to greater pollution of the environment[11]. Myrdal (1989-1987) said that in order to come to conclusions about the advantages of one system of distribution over another, "we must introduce value judgment from outside economics." He also linked economics with social science and political science[12]. Thus, we can conclude, with Zarqa, that Islamic economics consists of normative as well as positive judgments and that conventional economics are not free of value judgments and subjective assessments, particularly in choosing between alternatives or when interpreting results or analyzing an economic phenomenon[13].

Ethics and Economics

The relation between ethics and Islamic economics is found in the comprehensive nature of Islam incorporating the economic sphere; this is usually referred to as Muamalat (transactions), with Ibadat (worships). This link between Islam and economics imposes certain ethical values. These values prescribe:

(1) A way of conduct that reminds the Muslims that they should seek their reward in this life and the hereafter! The Qur'an says: "who has created life and death that he may try you, which of you is best in conduct, and he is the Mighty, the Forgiving" (67:2).

(2) Duties (Fara'yed) imposed on all Muslims. For example, a religious tax on wealth and income (Zakat), and the inheritance law.

(3) Halal (lawful) and haram (unlawful) acts. For instance, trade is an economic activity that is halal, whereas riba (usury) is a haram activity. It is contended that all halal activities lead to justice in the exchange process. All haram activities are forbidden because they lead to injustice and disputes. Ibn Taymiyah, an Islamic jurist, argues that Shari'a has imposed a restriction in those fields that are necessary for people's livelihood (e.g., sales, rent, gifts), banning that which inflicts harm and permitting that of social utility)[14].

Similarly, the Bible prescribes a way of conduct for believers and is not concerned only with spiritual matters. Theologians and reformers in the West have been concerned with ethics and values. For example, the concept of just price was explicitly tackled by Thomas Aquinas (1225-1274)[15]. Moreover, we should not forget the deliberations of many Christian scholars such as William of Ockham, who, in the 14th century, considered the will of God the determining factor of ethics and that "the divine command or prohibition [is that which] constitutes the rightness or wrongness of an action[16]." Thus Ockham's theory is very similar to the Islamic views about ethics noted above. Furthermore, ethics since the crisis of 2003 aims at placing the common good above individual ambition. The World Economic Forum has called upon governments to stress their human development index rather than their gross domestic products[17].

On the other hand, neoclassical economic theory does not concern itself with what is right or wrong. It views economic man as a person who seeks his own benefit, maximizing his own utility. This theory appears to be fading away. As Patriarch Bartholomew of Constantinople's said,

> We have an ethical responsibility to consider carefully the way that we inhabit the world and the life styles that we choose to adopt. The priorities and programs that we establish with regard to sustainable development and recycling eradicating biological and chemical waste addressing the problem of global and preserving our oceans, rivers and lakes reflect the genuine interest entrusted us by our creator.[18]

> A way of conduct that reminds the Muslims that they should seek their reward in this life and the hereafter! The Quran says, "Who has created life and death that he may try you, which of you is best in conduct, and He is the Mighty, the Forgiving" (67:2). The Messenger of God says, "The noblest of you are the best in character."[19]

The Economic Problem

In the opinion of the majority of Islamic authors and economists, the crux of the economic problem is found in poverty; the emphasis is less upon the scarcity of resources, since they invariably believe that God has created a universe full of resources. The duty of all races is to seek the bounties of Allah, who has provided them with natural wealth in a well-balanced measure. Hence Allah states,

> "Verily, all things have we created in proportion and measure" (54:49) and

> It is God who has created the heavens and the earth and sendeth down rain from the skies, and with it bringeth out fruits wherewith to feed you; it is He who hath made the ships subject to you, that they may sail through the sea by His command; and the rivers also hath He made subject to you. And He has made subject to you the sun and the moon, both diligently pursuing their courses; and the night and the day

hath He (also) made subject to you. And He giveth you of all
that you ask for, but if you count the favors of God, never will
ye be able to number them, verily man is given up to injustice
and ingratitude. (14:32, 33, 43)

Undoubtedly these verses are a revealing indication of Allah's
innumerable gifts. We should not, however, forget that the effective
exploitation of natural resources requires planning, knowledge, capital,
advanced technology, and, above all, entrepreneurial skills to help bring
about the efficient allocation of scarce resources to achieve growth and
progress. It is customary among Islamic authors to attribute the causes of
scarcity to injustice in distribution[1]. This is hardly convincing, particularly
in underdeveloped countries that are deprived of natural resources, skilled
manpower, and adequate capital. God says:" If God were to enlarge the
provision for His servents, They would indeed transgress." (42:27)

On the other hand, Western economists have cited scarcity and
inefficient allocation of resources as the main causes of economic problems,
as reflected in Robin's (1898-1984) definition: "Economics is the science
which studies human behavior as a relationship between ends and scarce
means which have alternative uses."[20] Ultimately, there should not be too
many differences between the Islamic and Western views with respect to
economic problems, since poverty is caused mainly by scarcity and scarcity
leads to poverty.

Endnotes

1. The above-mentioned explanation of the Islamic schools is based on M. Shaltout, *Al-Islam Aqidatun wa Sharia* [Islam, Conviction and a Law], Dar al-Shuruk, Beirut, 1983, pp. 506-550.
2. Muslim years are denoted by the letter *h.*
3. The origins of Islamic principles are summarized from the Arabic versions of the following references:
   1. a. Sobhi Mahmassani, *The Philosophy of Jurisprudence in Islam,* 5th ed., Dar El-Elm, Beirut, 1980, Passim: b.Abdul wahab Khalaf, *Origins of Islamic Jurisprudence,* Dar Al Kalam, Kuwait, 1978, Passim.
4. Ali Hayder, "Durar al Ahkam, Sharh Majallet al Ahkam," [Pearls of Rules, Explanation of Rules Magazine] Dar alkutub al Elmieh, Beirut, n.d.
5. S. M. Hasanuzzaman, "Definitions of Islamic Economics," *Journal of Research in Islamic Economics,* Vol. 1, No. 2, 1984, p. 52.
6. Baqr al-Sadr, *Iqtisaduna* [Our Economy], 3rd ed., Dar al-Taaruf, Beirut, 1980, p. 334.
7. Khurshid Ahmed, "Islamic Economics, Nature and Need," Journal of Research in Islamic EconomicsVol. 1, No. 2,.1984, p. 55. For criticism of this definition, see S. R. Khan, ibid, Vol. 2, No. 2, 1985, pp. 98-99.
8. The Age of Marshall: Aspects of British Economic Thought 1890-1915 by Narma deshwar jha, London:F Case, 1973
9. The Macmillan Company (1932). Robbins headed the London School of Economics in 1929.
10. Among this group of classical economists are also Alfred Marshall and A.C. Pigou.
11. Robert Heilbroner, "Economic, How Scientific?" *Economic Impact,* No. 2, p. 55, cited in M. Saqr in the First Conference on al-Iqtisad al Islami, (Conference on Research in Islamic Economics, 1980, pp. 38-40.
12. Gunnar Myrdal, *The Political Element in the Development of Economic Theory,* New Jersey: Transaction Publishing 2nd ed., 2004.
13. Anas Zarqa, "Islamic Economics: An Approach to Human Welfare," in K. Ahmad, Jeddah: King AbdulAziz university. Ed., 1980, pp. 3-18.
14. See Ibn Taymiyah, "Al Qawa'ed al-Nourania al-Fiqhiyah,"(The enlighten Jurisprudence Rules) in A. Al-Khateeb, *Monetary Policy in Islam,* Dar al-Nahda, Cairo, 1961, p. 113.
15. John E Bell, *A History of Economic Thought,* New York: Ronald Press, 1953*p.* 346, and R. Wilson, *Banking and Finance in the Arab Middle East,* Macmillan, London, 1983, p. 70.

16. W. L. Reese, *Dictionary of Philosophy and Religion, Eastern and Western Thought*, Humanities Press, New Jersey, 1980, p. 157.
17. Values and Ethics: Insights from the Orthodox Christian Tradition," Report on Faith and the Global Agenda. Values for the Post-Crisis Economy. World Economic Forum, Klaus Schwab, Geneva, 2010, pp. 19-20.
18. "Values in the Post Crisis Economy," Report of the World Economic Forum, op. cit., p. 21.
19. El-Gousi, 1982, p. 19, and A. Haykal, *Madkhal ila al Iqtisad al Islami [Introduction to Islamic Economy]*, Dar al-Nahda al-Arabieh, Beirut, pp. 47-50.
20. See Philip A. S. Taylor, *A New Dictionary of Economics*, Rutledge and Kegan Paul, London, 1966, pp. 78-88.

CHAPTER 3

Wealth Its Source and Ownership in Islam

The concept of wealth and ownership in Islam provides a revealing portrait of Islamic philosophy and shows how the Islamic ideology is interwoven throughout economics. The following passages attempt to explain the theory of wealth and property in Islam, focusing on their foundation and origin, the rights and limitation of ownership, public versus private ownership, and types of property.

The theory of wealth in Islam is based on certain principles but especially the principle that God is the creator and owner of wealth and human beings (*al-Insan*) are merely the vicegerents of God.[1] Of creation, it is said: "We have enabled the sons of Adam, carried them on land and sea, nurtured them with lawful enjoyment, and preferred them to much of our creation" (5:76). God's ownership of creation is also stressed: "To Him belongs what is in the Heavens and on Earth and all between them, and all beneath the soil" (20:6).

The Quran considers possession of wealth a "trying test." God says,

> It is He who has made you (His) agents, inheritors of the earth; He has raised you in ranks, some above others; that He may try you in the gifts He has given you. Verily, your Lord is quick in punishment, yet He is indeed oft forgiving, Most Merciful. (6:165)

On the other hand, many verses of the Quran stress that *al-Insan* is an owner of his wealth in the form of a mandate or trusteeship:

Believe in God and His Messenger, and spend (in charity) out of the (substance), whereof He has made you heirs. For those of you who believe and spend (in charity) for them there is a great reward. And what cause have you why you should not spend in the cause of God? For to God belongs the heritage of the heavens and the earth. (57:5, 7, 10)

Careful analysis and a thorough understanding of Islamic principles lead us to believe that there is no contradiction between these verses and those cited earlier. The second phenomenon (man as vicegerent) is but a natural sequel emanating from and interrelated with the first phenomenon (God is the creator and owner). God has simply chosen *al-Insan* to be his trustee on earth and subjected "to him all what is on Heaven and on Earth." Thus, God is the donor and man is the beneficiary. This unique relationship entails certain rights and encompasses certain obligations and duties that must be literally adhered to by the beneficiary.

Wealth Source and Knowledge

The Prophet emphasized the importance of both wealth and knowledge. In His words,

There shall be no envy but in two cases: The person whom Allah has given wealth and power to spend in the service of truth and the person whom Allah has granted knowledge of things and he judges by it or teaches to others.[2]

This equalization of wealth and knowledge leads us to believe that wealth is attained separately such from inheritance and donation by knowledgeable people. On the other hand, such learned persons must work hard to gain and prosper.

Ownership Rights and Duties

God entrusted man with property and wealth and organized the way man may utilize his right: "Do not cover the bounties which God has bestowed more abundantly on some of you than on others" (4:32). Rights of ownership comprise the right of possession, utilization, and disposition of one's property and must be exercised in a manner acceptable to God:

1. The right of possession entails certain obligations on the part of the possessor, including the protection and safeguard of property against loss or damage (that may be caused by negligence, misappropriation or reckless spending), and more importantly the enlargement of ones property or wealth. Sound investment management and continuous endeavors to enlarge one's property are seen as serving not only the owner, but also society as well. God says, "Spend [on others] out of sustenance we have granted them" (2:3) and "Behold, the pious [who] in their property acknowledge a due share [*huq*] to those who ask and to those who are deprived" (51:14-18).

2. The right of utilization embraces the enjoyment and benefit of property. The Quran says, "Men shall have the benefit of what they earn, and women shall have the benefit of what they earn" (4:43). At the same time, the owner is required to avoid extravagance, reckless spending, usury, and hoarding. In addition, the Quran imposes the obligation to avoid improper utilization through wrongful acts such as gambling, drinking, consuming drugs, and all types of betting.

3. The right of disposition entitles the owner to transfer his ownership during his life through selling and buying, donations and grants, and inheritance after his death. Emphasizing this, the Prophet declared openly in his farewell speech, "Hear me, O my nation! Live together but do not do wrong, do not do wrong! For taking the property of a man is not permissible except by his finding it good [*bi-tibi nafsin minhu*]."[3]

These duties and obligations forbid the owner from deviating from the inheritance rules set forth in the Quran and Shari'a (see Inheritance Law section).

How Property Is Acquired

Property rights are recognized by the Quran and the Prophet's tradition: "Whosoever takes a piece of wealth by force from another man shall meet his Lord and He will be angry with him."[4]

The Prophet also said, "Who is killed while trying to save and protect his property is a martyr."[5]

> Private property is acquired through several lawful means, either as a result of one's own effort;
> by contractual relationship through ordinary business transactions;
> by inheritance, donation, or
> grants (*iqta'h*); or by preemption rights. It is haram to acquire property by unlawful means
> as in coercion, fraud, stealing, cheating, and gambling or to knowingly buy stolen property.

Limitations on Property Rights

Essentially, there is no quantitative limitation on the desired or optimal accepted volume of property or wealth to be owned by the individual. The Prophet stated, "What an excellent thing is lawfully earned wealth in the hands of a good man."[6] However, there are certain exceptions according to well-established rules of Islamic jurisprudence stressing that "necessities make forbidden things allowed."[7]

These necessities could be numerous and included the case of famine. Islam urges people to share and sacrifice their individual belongings for the interest of the whole community.

After a famine struck the nation, Caliph Omar was reported as saying, "If (the famine) lasts one year I would add to every household their equivalent number, for people will not suffer on half rations" (literally with a half-filled stomach).[8] We can say that the marginal utility of the first few units of food one consumes is very high, since these units are essential to sustain life. If an individual who has 10 units is willing to give away five to the needy, his marginal utility will surely be affected. However, the loss of five units for an individual who owns 50 units is hardly noticeable and causes no harm, as explained by Caliph Omar. The same principle holds should the community suffer from a scarcity of essential food and provisions, as once happened while the Prophet was traveling with His companions. The Prophet said, "Whoever has a surplus of provisions should give to a person who has nothing, and whoever has a surplus animal for riding shall give to a person who has no horse."[9]

Public versus Private Property

This last hadith has prompted some Islamic authors to conclude that private ownership is not recognized in Islam until everyone's minimum subsistence level has been attained.[10] Some authors believe that public property in Islam is preeminent and not be subordinate to private property.[11] Having looked into this matter, Islam recognizes four kinds of property: private, common or joint ownership, and state property.

Common property includes roads, highways, rivers, and mosques. State property can include the Treasury (Beit al-Mal) and government buildings and installations. Property may not be restricted to a particular person's use, denying others. Likewise, a ruler is not allowed to keep property for himself or his closest aide or any other private owner.[12] A controversy concerning minerals has arisen among scholars regarding non-apparent minerals, which includes any metalthat requires further work and development in its extraction. If such resources exist on private property, there were two schools of thought as to its ownership: One school holds that the owner of the land can extract the minerals and keep four-fifths of the yield and pay 20% as *rikaz*.[13] The second school, particularly the Malikis, holds that the land's ownership should be transferred to public property. Nevertheless, the original owners are entitled to fair compensation.[14]

Conclusion

Private property in Islam is well protected and maintained. The owner has a social obligation toward the community and other obligations toward God (the donor). State and public property seek to serve society and provide for public utilities and necessities. Neither form of property should impinge on the other. In cases of conflict, public interest comes before private interest. Nationalization is not an objective and may only be exercised for the public good on the condition that the initial owners are fairly compensated and that the individual's motivation or incentives are not impaired. To safeguard peoples' incentives, Islam protects private property and urges Muslims to develop their wealth and investments without harm or injury toward society. By following the precepts of Islam, harm and injury can be eliminated and brotherhood and cooperation established.

Endnotes

1. This is different from a *viceregent*, which means a regent's deputy; *vicegerent* means "any bishop or priest, considered the earthly deputy of God or Christ." See Taylor, *A New Dictionary of Economics*, op cit.
2. Ibn Hanbal (d. 241-855)," Musnad al Imam Ahmad b Hanba", Cairo: al Maktaba yamamiyeh 1895, reprint al matba'ah al islamiyah, 1978. The Quran also says, "Eat of the good things which God hath provided for you lawful and good; but fear God, in whom ye believe" (5:91; see also 5:90, 6:141).
3. Narrated by Ibn Hanbal and Ibn Maja.
4. Narrated by Ahmed;
5. Reported by El-Bukhari in A. W. Wafi, "Economic Integration in Islam," Sixth Conference of the Academy of Islamic Research (AIR), Cairo, 1971, p. 768.
6. Reported by El-Bukhari, op. cit., p. 769, and in al-Sebaii, 1960, p. 131.
7. M. Kah'f, "Taxation Policy and Resource Allocation," in Z. Ahmed (Ed.), Jeddah: CRIE and Institue if and Instiute if Policy Studies, 1983, p. 146.
8. Quoted in Al-Jammal, Muhammad Abdul Munim," Mawsu at Al-Iqtisad Al-Islami" Dar Al-Kitab Al-Misri, Cairo: 1980, p182.
9. Reported by Muslim in "al-Iqtisad al-Islami," *Journal of Research in Islamic Economics*, 1980, p. 141.
10. Al-Finjari, M Sh, Towards an Islamic Economy, Dar OKAZ, Jeddah, 1981. p.128. As reported by Abu Dawoud, to support his views. Al-Finjari cited the Prophet: "Should a believer sleep hungry, nobody's money is his along."
11. AL-Awadi, R, Distribution Theory in an Islamic Economy (Arabic) Cairo, Al-Azhar, 1974.p. 313.
12. *al-Umm*, Kitab al-Shaab, Vol. 2, Cairo, al dar al Kawmieh, 1968, p. 131
13. *Rikaz* is a tax on hidden treasures.
14. Al-Sadr, op. cit., 1980, pp. 499-508, for a detailed discussion.

CHAPTER 4

Labor and Productivity

This chapter discusses the meaning and importance of work, the concept of wages, the rights and duties of employees/workers, and work ethics in Islam. "Islam stands for social justice based on productive labor and equal opportunities so that everyone can work according to his ability and reaps the fruits of his work."[1] In this respect, God says, "Never will I suffer to be lost the work of any of you, be he male or female" (5:195).

Work and productivity in the Islamic teachings are a divine duty. In Islam worship is not restricted to praying, fasting, paying alms, and pilgrimage but also includes performing one's job to the best of one's ability. More so, "the one who renders a useful service to people is in fact extending a kind of charity for which he will be rewarded."[2] In addition, Islamic jurists have stated that it is a religious obligation of Muslims to try to provide for a happy life for themselves and society.

The fact that work is a divine act implies that it is a duty ordained on all capable men and women and an honor without which a person is deemed unproductive. By contrast, work and productivity enhance progress, give meaning to life, and makes people worthy. The Prophet said, "Work is no disgrace, it is idleness which is a disgrace" and "The best labors are gaining from a lawful livelihood."[3] Ibn Khaldoun once wrote, "Earnings (from work) are the value of human labor,"[4] implying that idle labor has no positive value since it does not contribute to any increase in output. Wages are to be determined by the type of work performed in conjunction with a fair market rate and by observing the principle of equal work for equal pay. The payment of wages should not be unduly delayed. For piecemeal jobs, wages are normally due upon completion of the work. In God's words,

"And O my people! Neither give just measure and weight nor withhold from the people the things that are their due" (11:85). The Prophet said, "Give the worker his wages before his sweat dries."[5]

The employer-worker relationship is characterized by justice and brotherhood. Incorporating these principles in the marginal utility function, one could say that the marginal utility of an employer (e.g., a factory owner) is determined by the renter's income and the wages of his worker on the basis of justice and equity. By the same token, the marginal utility of the laborer is a function of his wages and the amount of rent he is able to generate for his employer.[6] Thus the marginal utilities of both the laborer and the employer/owner in the Islamic economy are interdependent on each other's welfare, as in conventional economics, in accordance with Pareto optimality.

The Wage System versus the Sharing System

Profit and loss sharing, as outlined in this book can be extended to labor/employer contracts. However the Islamic literature has not rigorously addressedthe wage system versus the sharing systemAt this stage, our aim is to briefly emphasize that the sharing system has its roots in the Islamic market and that this system could substitute for the existing wage system in industry and serve to promote small business in Islamic countries, including Kuwait. Since young Arabs, particularly in the Gulf countries, regard wage labor as degrading and usually refuse to work on an assembly line, we realize the importance of the sharing system in solving this problem, as indicated by UDOVITCH₃₇

From the Geniza documents it is apparent that a form of economic collaboration was eschewed since dependence upon others for livelihood was considered degrading and humiliating. Consequently many enterprises, no matter how modest a scale, requiring the combined efforts of more than one person would be organized in the form of partnership and commended as [mudaraba.

The sharing system in Islamic countries can encompass a combination of wages and industry profit sharing. The system has various merits: First, the worker must earn a minimum wage to sustain a living and support his family[8]. Without this minimum, the workers/labor would not have the required incentive to participate in the scheme. Second, the idea of profit creates the necessary motivation and reduces enforcement costs. Third, during a depression, profit distribution may be cut, as opposed to workers being laid off. More significantly, the scheme provides the necessary impetus for young workers to work in industry. This policy reduces dependence on foreign labor and creates more jobs for fresh graduates from technical schools and/or colleges.

Work Ethics in Islam

The Islamic tradition tries to eliminate moral hazard problems by emphasizing that workers' and employers' duties are no less important than their rights. For example, they should abide by the following work ethics 1) honesty and righteousness, for Allah says, "It is not your wealth nor your sons that will bring you nearer to us in degree, but only those who believe and work righteousness these are the ones for whom there is a multiplied reward" (34:37), see also (18:30), 2) perfection, for the Prophet is reported as saying, "Verily Allah likes you when you make something to make it with perfection"[9]

3) fulfilling one's obligations, as in "Ye who believe! Fulfill all obligations" (5:1), and 4) an employer should never request a laborer to work beyond his capacities, for "on no soul doth God place a burden greater than it can bear" (2:286).

Favoritism is also strongly condemned by the Prophet: "He who puts a man in charge of a team though there is better than him, he betrayed Allah, his messenger and all believers."[10] In addition, an employer is required to offer equal opportunities to all workers, for Islam advocates perfect competition in the labor market. Accordingly, it is forbidden for monopolistic or monopsonic employers to carry out monopolistic actions on the supply side Likewise, the labor unions' actions to restrict entry of labor to particular occupations to keep wages up in the face of declining demand violates the liberty of non-unionists to work. Furthermore, it dampens the principle of equality and equal opportunities for workers irrespective of age, sex, creed, race, or affiliation. This raises two questions: one concerning the powers and authorities of unions in the Islamic setting and the second concerning the effects of dismantling monopolistic practices on the transfer payments of workers. Both these issues have yet to be explored by Islamic economists.

Ethics in Contract and Commercial Transactions

Both the Quran and Sunna urge honesty, the fulfillment of contracts, and probity. Many section of the Quran urge believers to weigh with true balance: "This will be [for your own good] and best in the end" (17:35). Furthermore,

> The Messenger of God passed by a heap of foodstuff. He thrust his hand into it, and his fingers encountered dampness. He said, "What is this, o owner of foodstuff?" The merchant said, "O Messenger of God, rain has stricken it." The Prophet replied, "Why do you not put it at the top of the foodstuff, so that the people may see it? He who deceives is not of me."[11]

The Prophet also warned,

> Do not meet al-jalab [i.e., meet outside the town those who drive animals from one place to another for sale], the master of the one who is met, and is purchased from has an option when he comes to the market[12].

On fulfilling contracts, the Quran says, "Oh you who believe! Fulfill all contracts [uqud]." Vogel and Hayes commented that addressing those who believe reveals that the fulfillment of contracts is part and parcel of faith[13]: "God commands you to deliver your trust [amanat] to those entitled to them" (4:58).

Similarly, the Prophet said, "The Muslims are bound by their stipulations [shuritihin]."[14] Another hadith states, "If a man makes a promise he must fulfill it." The Prophet forbade loans and sales in a single contract: "Illicit are a loan and a sale [salaf wa-bay'] or two stipulations in a sale, or sale of what you do not have."[15] "Delay by a solvent person is sin and may be punished as a crime." Finally, the merchant is highly respected by the Prophet, who said, "A faithful and trustworthy merchant is said to be with the Prophets on the Day of Judgment."

Endnotes:

1. See Resolutions of the Third Conference of the AIR, 1966, p. 544.
2. Sheikh M. Abu Zahra, "Human Society. Under the Aegis of Islam," Third Conference of the AIR, 1966, p. 433.
3. Cited in Al-Najjar, ibid p. 28.
4. Abdul-Hady al-Najjar, *Islam and Economics (Al-Islam and Al-Iqtisad)*, Aalam al-Ma'arefet, Kuwait, 1983, pp. 20-40.
5. Cited in El-Gousi, op. cit., p. 35.
6. M. A.Choudry, Principles of Islamic Economics", Middle Eastern Studies, pp 96-7
7. Op cit, 1970, p 184.
8. The same views are expressed by Islamic authors; for example, see Hakim Said, *The Employer and the Employee, the Islamic Concept*, Motamar al-Alam al-Islami, Karachi, 1965. For Western advocates, see Bert L Metzger, *Evolution of the Profit-Sharing/Share Ownership Philosophy Worldwide*, Profit Sharing Research Foundation, Evanston, Illinois, 1980.
9. Narrated by Al-Baihaqi: Y. al-Qrdawi, *Faith and Life*, al-Dar al-Saudiah, Jeddah, 1969, p. 303.
10. Imam Al-Hafez (d. 656 h), *Al-Targhib wa Tarheeb*, Vol. II, 4th ed., Cairo, Ministry of Awkaf, 1980, p. 138.
11. Narrated by Muslim.
12. Narrated by Muslim.
13. Ibid.
14. Narrated by Abu Dawud, al Tirmidhi.
15. Narrated by Abu Dawud, al Tirmidhi.

CHAPTER 5

The Islamic Distribution System and Social Justice

slam stands firmly for justice in all aspects of life. "God commands justice, the doing of good, and liberality to kith and kin and He forbids all shameful deeds, and injustice and rebellion: He instructs you that you may receive admonition" (16:90). The Islamic concept of social justice aims to provide equal opportunities for all persons capable of earning a living. Primarily, ownership, labor, and need are the three basic elements of the Islamic distribution system. This chapter discusses the principles and policies of social justice, with a particular emphasis on the constituents of need in Islam, followed by means of distribution. The focus is therefore upon zakat, inheritance law, and land distribution. Labor and ownership are discussed later in the chapter.

Justice and equality in Islam require that people have a fair opportunity and do not imply that they should be equal in poverty or in riches. The Quran says, "God will raise up to (suitable) ranks (and degrees) those of you who believe and who have been granted knowledge, and God is well acquainted with all you do" (58:11). Although individuals are not equal in status, wealth, or knowledge, they are equal before God and the best among them are the most pious (see (49:13)). However, it is incumbent on the Islamic state to provide the basic needs or primary necessities to its citizens. Its primary purpose is to moderate social variances in Islamic society and enable the poor to lead a normal spiritual and material life, in dignity and contentment.

According to Sayed Qutb, social justice in Islam is a "humane justice" aiming at instituting fairness in all values and not merely economic ones.[1] For instance, it is unfair to give social benefits to a healthy or young individual who is lazy and unwilling to work, for the Prophet says,

"It is better for a person to take his rope and bind wood than beseech people for charity, immaterial whether they respond or refuse."[2]

The minimum subsistence level is actually a minimum guaranteed income. This income can be earned completely through labor, partially earned, or given in entirety by the Beit al-Mal (the Treasury). In the latter case the transfer payment should be sufficient to secure a minimum standard of living for recipients who have no other income. The minimum standard of living varies from country to country and depends on the community's degree of wealth and the Treasury's available resources. This point is important since it sheds light on the differences between the Islamic welfare system and other systems. In socialist and capitalist systems, the state is totally responsible for generating the revenue necessary to cover this social cost. The revenue may be generated from direct and indirect taxes or through deficit financing in accordance with the government's fiscal policies.

In the Islamic system, the community, represented by those who have more than the requisite *nisab* (threshold), shares the burden of providing the guaranteed minimum income to the needy under the supervision of the Beit al-Mal. *Nisab* is defined as the residual minimum level of income sufficient to meet the necessities of one family for one year.[3] Naturally, the state covers the shortage should the collection one year fall below the required budget. The majority of jurists define primary necessities as the minimum subsistence level sufficient to provid food, clothing, shelter, medical care, education, and a servant (for the disabled). Al Shatibi adds to this list other social services, such as transportation.[4] Ali bin Abi Taleb, the fourth caliph, describes necessities as that which prevents hunger, nakedness, and hardship.[5]

Distribution Tools and Their Economic Objectives

As emphasized in the Holy Quran, the objective of an economic system is to distribute the wealth produced in a manner, "so that it may not circulate only between the rich among you" (59:7). However, the free market economy and planned economies have failed so far to equally distribute wealth among their citizens. For instance, in the United States 20% of the people owned almost 85% of all privately held wealth.[6] The distribution of wealth is a primary issue in Islamic economics and is manifested in three systems, namely, the distribution of wealth and income which aims to achieve social justice, the distribution of natural resources, and the system of social and economic solidarity.[7] The central theme in these systems is to prevent the concentration of wealth, decrease the cost of social services provided by the state, and foster solidarity and caring in society.

There are three vital elements in distribution: zakat, inheritance law, and the distribution of land. Distributional means besides awkaf are discussed in previous sections of this chapter[8] and include the following.

1. The system of distributing wealth and income, which mainly includes zakat, religious endowments (awkaf), gifts, zakat *al-fit'r* (charity enjoined on most Muslims, including those below the poverty line but who can afford to donate a token of their daily income once a year), *Fay'* (distribution of land gained by peaceful means), *rikaz* (minerals and metals), and treasure. God says,

    > What God has bestowed on his Apostle and taken away from the people of the towns, belongs to God, to *His Apostle* and to Kindred and Orphans, the needy and the wayfarer; in order that it may not (merely) make a circuit between the wealthy among you. (59:7)

2. The system of distributing natural resources, which mainly includes joint participation in certain categories of wealth (e.g., water, pasture, and forestry), the provision of surplus water or surplus natural resources by those who have it to those who do not, land cultivation and *Iqta'h* (allocating barren land for cultivation).
3. A system of compulsory economic solidarity, including debtors' shares of zakat revenue and the shares of wayfarers, compulsory obligations toward one's family, the provision of the bare minimum for subsistence by the state to every citizen, and the right to obtain the sufficient minimum (defined as clothing, food, shelter, and medical treatment).

The following section discusses the economic implications of zakat, land distribution, and inheritance law and awkaf.[9]

The Role of Zakat in Distribution

Zakat is considered the third pillar (*rokn*) of Islam, the other pillars are professions of faith, prayer (*salat*), zakat, fasting (*sawm*), and pilgrimage to

Makkah (*al haj*). In a way, Zakat is an act of worship requiring the believer to relinquish a portion of his wealth or income for the benefit of the poor. In this sense, it varies from prayer (also an act of worship) in that the latter does not require a sacrifice other than the time spent in praying. In contrast, zakat requires sacrificing part of one's current income as well as accumulated wealth. According to the first Caliph Abu Bakr Al-Siddiq, "Zakat is a claim against wealth."[10] Specifically it was levied on apparent and non-apparent wealth, such land and fruit, cattle, mining products, gold and silver, and articles of trade, all items that constituted elements of wealth in the early days of Islam. However, zakat rates range from 2.5% on idle cash balances, articles of trade, silver, and gold, except jewelry for ornamental and personal use, to, for example, 5% on products of irrigated land, 20% on minerals and treasures extracted from the earth, and 1% ushr) on agricultural land watered by rainfall.[11]

Zakat Characteristics and Fiscal Policy

Having established that zakat is almsgiving ordained by God and not an ordinary tax, it follows that zakat is not and was never meant to be a tool of fiscal policy. Though similar to taxes, since both have a rate levied on a certain base (income, assets, or likewise), it differs in many ways. Although zakat possesses certain properties that make it desirable, it is beyond the control of the fiscal authorities, as shown here.

1. Zakat is an ordinance levy aimed at purifying both the individual and the capital wealth, as revealed in the Quran (Tawbeh, p. 103).
2. In addition to an act of worship, zakat is an "expression of gratitude to Allah for having bestowed the bounties on the individual"[12] and, in God's words,

> A token unto them is the dead earth, we revive it, and we bring forth from it grain so that they eat thereof. And we have placed therein gardens of the date-palm and grapes, and we have caused springs of water to gush forth therein . . . will they not then give thanks. (36:33-55)

3. Collection and distribution of zakat are the duty of the state within the limits prescribed by the Quran. Its rates are standard (flat) and this

rigidity prevents it from being utilized as a stabilizing factor in fiscal policy.

4. Recipients of zakat are explicitly mentioned in the Quran; thus its distribution is not left to the discretion of the fiscal authorities. The Quranic verse cites,

> Alms are for the poor and the needy, and those employed to administer the (fund) for those whose hearts have been (recently) reconciled (to truth). For those in bondage and in debt; in the cause of God; and for the wayfarer; (thus it is) ordained by God, and God is full of knowledge and wisdom. (9:60)

5. The divine law and the tradition of the Prophet and his companions introduced several principles for zakat collection and administration 14 centuries ago. These principles were innovative at that time and are essential features of modern tax legislation and include the following.

   1. The principle of matching certain types of revenues with certain types of expenditure. For example, zakat revenue must be distributed among certain categories of recipients. Lewis, for instance, recommended the "earmarking" of a "tax on wages" for the benefit of a social security fund.[13]
   2. The principles of minimum exemption limit, the *nisab* (threshold).
   3. The principle of fairness or the ability to pay, for example, those with wealth or income in excess of the *nisab* are considered able to pay and those with wealth or income below or equal to the *nisab* are exempt.
   4. The principle that no tax should be levied twice on the same basis (i.e., the prohibition of double taxation).
   5. The zakat levy can be in cash or in kind, depending upon the zakat base. In this respect, it represents a flow of goods and services from the rich to the poor defined as a "progressive transfer."[14]

Economic Implications of Zakat

In essence, the economic implications of zakat are the following.

1. The creation of purchasing power among the recipients, thus raising their consumption if distributed in cash. As Kahf (noted,

the distribution of zakat increases the disposable income of the recipients.[15] This raises demand in the economy, provided the zakat receiver's marginal propensity to consume exceeds that of the zakat donor.

2. The redistribution of wealth and income through the mobilization of idle resources by an amount equivalent to the tax levy. For instance, when zakat is levied on unexploited land, personal jewelry, or idle cash balances, it can lead to the gradual transfer of wealth from idle owners to more dynamic recipients.[16] "This argument"? differs from that of Volker Nienhaus, who tried to understate the effect of zakat on growth and mobilization on the grounds that it does not change the amount of wealth.

3. Encouraging investment, since it is a tax on accumulated net wealth rather than a tax on income alone. The Prophet said, "Invest the orphans' capital so that it may not be wiped out by zakat."[17] However, if we consider the case where zakat is levied on barren land at 10% (usher) per year, we can say that the land will be gradually transferred from the original idle owner to presumably more dynamic recipient(s). The expected exploitation by the new owner ultimately increases society's wealth and output. This is supported by the fact that zakat revenue was estimated at 3-3.6% of the gross national product in Syria and Sudan in 1971 and 1982, respectively.[18]

4. Discouraging hoarding and establishing a society based on brotherhood, cooperation, and solidarity, which ultimately leads to the prevention of class war.

5. Subsidizing the poor, thus decreasing the burden of the fiscal authorities and freeing government revenue for other productive projects.

Al-Hima'h and Land Allocation

The Prophet instituted a new system whereby the state can allocate a piece of government land (called Hima'h land). This land is protected by the ruler for the benefit of society, to be used mainly for horse grazing in previous centuries. Land thus became the property of the masses and, consequently, private ownership of Hima'h land was banned. The Prophet also allocated barren land to certain Muslims. It then became a tradition to give a title of ownership to those who actively cultivated the land for three consecutive years. The Prophet said, "Land belongs to Allah and the human beings too. Whoever rehabilitates barren land becomes its owner; no holder has a right after three years."[19] On another occasion Caliph Omar allocated a piece of land for grazing for the cattle of the poor and banned wealthy landlords from using the same plot. His argument was that landlords could always fall back and live on their cultivated land should their cattle die from a lack of grazing land. By contrast, the poor cattle owners had no land and it seems fair to provide them with necessary food and other provisions.[20]

The incidents cited reveal the economic necessity that dictates them. They also reveal a spirit of cooperation and brotherhood that is further illustrated in the following three points.

1. Irrigated land was very rare in the Arabian Desert and still is, thus calling for exceptional measures to induce small farmers and particularly the underprivileged to revive barren land.
2. The distribution of land for cultivation or Hima'h purposes is for the public good. In rare cases the government may acquire private land for distribution, provided the initial owners are compensated at the going market price. However, general contention favors the distribution of government or no-man's land over private ownership.

Accordingly, it must be on the outskirts of a town and its possession or holding should be authorized by the Imam (ruler).[21]

3. The Shari'a principle behind this issue states, "A private injury is tolerated to ward off a public injury.[22]"

Evidently, the distribution of barren land has far-reaching economic consequences. Apart from distributing wealth, it fosters economic development and creates an opportunity to own land for those willing to and capable of work.

The Inheritance Law

The inheritance law is another aspect of the Islamic distribution system. By this law, Islam seeks to redistribute wealth and establish justice and equality in the distribution of ownership. The significance of the law lies in the fact that its foundations, including the method of distribution, are based on well-devised criteria. These foundations were long been established in the Quran and are still applicable today, a revealing indication of their solid basis:

> "God (thus) directs you [in] regards [to] your children's (inheritance): to the male, a portion equal to that of two females; if only daughters, two or more, their share is two-thirds of the inheritance; if only one, her share is a half. For parents, a sixth share of the inheritance to each, if the deceased left children; if no children and the parents are, the (only) heirs, the mother has a third; if the deceased left brothers (or sisters) the mother has a sixth. The distribution in all cases is after the payment of legacies and debts. Ye know not whether your parents or your children are nearest to you in benefit. These are settled portions ordained by God, and God is all knowing, all wise. In what your wives leave, your share is a half, if they leave no child; but if they leave a child, ye get a fourth, after payment of legacies and debts. In what you leave, their share is a fourth, if ye leave no child, but if ye leave a child they get an eighth, after payment of legacies and debts.
>
> If the man or woman whose inheritance is in question has left neither ascendants nor descendants, but left a brother or a sister, each one of the two gets a sixth but if more than two they share in a third after payment of legacies and debts, so that no loss is caused (to anyone). Thus it is ordained by God; and God is all knowing, most forbearing. (4:11, 12)

Eligibility for inheritance is based on the following criteria. First, on the relationship of kinship and marriage,

1. Kinship generating through birth permits children to inherit from their parents and vice versa.
2. A marriage permits a husband to inherit from his wife and vice versa.

Second, children have an absolute right to inheritance, regardless of their age or sex. Third, brothers and sisters cannot inherit a deceased brother's or sister's property while their parents are alive. Fourth, a boy receives double the share of his sister.

The aforementioned principles are not without merit. Since inheritance is a transformation of wealth from the deceased to the heirs, it would be fair and equitable to have the nearest of kin as the lawful heir rather than an outsider.

Islam thus aims to strengthen family ties and eliminate family feuds and discord. However, the benefactor (or benefactress) is allowed to dispose of up to one-third of his/her property for the poor and distant relatives who are not eligible for inheritance. In this regard, the Prophet says

> "You may will away a third, but that is a lot. To leave your heirs rich is better than to leave them poor and begging from people. You will not spend anything, seeking thereby to please God, without being rewarded for it, even the mouthful you give your wife"[23].

The allocation of shares takes into consideration both need and obligation. This is why children have a greater share than their grandfathers, because their needs are greater although their degree of kinship (to the deceased) is similar. In addition, the male heir receives double the share of a female because, according to Shari'a, men are responsible for the welfare of their wives, daughters, and sisters, even if the women are rich or financially self-sufficient[24]. Besides, if a man leaves no heir other than one sister, she inherits one-half of the inheritance, and if he leaves two sisters, they inherit two-thirds (Quran 4:176).

Awkaf (Charitable Endowments)

The first benevolent cash waqf appeared approximately during 827/1423, when Haj Muslih Al Deen donated several shops in addition to 10,000 Agjah (cash money) to spend the return on Quran readers in a mosque in Aderna, Turkey. According to the donors, the return on these assets consisted of the shops' rentals and the yield received on lending the cash money at a fixed profit of 10%. Interestingly enough, this seem in violation of what we have already concluded. Further, the subject matter becomes even more intriguing when one realizes that Sheikh Al Islam Mullah Khasraf (1460-1480) wrote in his book *Durar al-Alhkam fi Shar'h*

Ghurar Al-Ahkam that Mohammad Al-Hassan Al Shaibani (d. 186/805) accepted movable waqf (*waqf al-Manqul*) based on Tasaruf rule also sanctioned by Zufar (d. 158/775), Imam Abu Hanife's student.

This raises an important question surrounding the difference between cash waqf and movable asset waqf. In Imam Zufar's opinion, the two are similar. Furthermore, the first is another type of movable asset waqf. However, this view was contested by Ibrahim b Mussa Al-Tarabulsi Al-Hanafi, who displayed the traditional stance of *al Salaf* regarding cash waqf. According to al-Tarabulsi, Muhammad b. Abdullah al-Ansari, a follower of Imam Zufar, approved cash waqf conditional upon paying the capital sum as *mudaraba* investment and recommending the donation of any excess to charity[25].

Nevertheless, dependence on investing cash waqf in *mudaraba* was limited due to the risk involved, since profits are not guaranteed. Consequently Rab Al-*Mal* (capital owner) have suffered losses that could have ultimately led to losing the capital itself. In spite of the restrictions on cash waqf by Al-Tarabulsi, mixed waqf (fixed and cash) gained popularity in Aleppo through wali Hallab Mohammad Basha during 963/1556 and in Salam during the reign of Suleiman al Kamuni (1520-1566). At least 65 cases of cash waqf were known, consisting of around 50% of benevolent waqf established in Jerusalem during the first and second centuries of Ottoman rule.

Upon examining the objectives of Shari'a in the preceding passages, we notice the emphasis on preserving the well-being of Muslims as humans. This can only be achieved through caring for and protecting individuals and the welfare system provided by the state of Islam and society. This system is unique in the following:

1. Its attribution to spiritual and man-made laws.
2. Society's contribution in financing and managing a huge part of this system.

Hence, the public sector is able to finance a sizable portion of the state's expenditures by calling upon various sources such as states' taxes, zakat collection, inheritance revenue, donations (*sadaqat*), *awqaf* proceedings, and so forth. On the other hand, the private sector contributes through benevolent *waqf* consisting of public or family endowments for the underprivileged, poor, and needy. Undoubtedly, the role of both public and private waqf is significant and reflected in caring for poor families, orphans (e.g., supplying them milk), widowers, divorced women, and the elderly and in providing homes for men and respected homeless women with no relatives or independent sources of income. Awqaf also takes care of marriages among young girls and allocates monthly stipends to the elderly and sick.

Specific Types of *Awqaf*

Specific types of *awqaf* include supplying shops, stores, clinics, mosques, agricultural land, mills, schools, bakeries, libraries, lighthouses, apartments, barren land, vegetables, and so forth.

Endnotes:

1. Sayed Qutb, *Social Justice in Islam*, Dar al Shuruk, Beirut, 1983, p. 28.
2. Mohammed El-Fahham, Grand Sheikh of Al-Azhar, "Social Reform between Two Extremes," SixthAIR Conference, Cairo, 1971, p. 680.
3. The major transfer payment (or distribution system) in the Islamic system is called zakat.
4. M. Kahf, "Fiscal Policy and Resource Allocation," in Ahmad, Ziauddin, et al, Ed, Fiscal Policy and Resource Allocation in Islam, Jeddah, CRIE & Institute of Policy Studies, 1983, p. 148
5. Ibid., p. 148.
6. G. William, Dunhoft, in Usmani, op. cit., p. 5.
7. -Anas Zarqa, "The System of Distribution in Islam," *Journal of Research in Islamic Economics*, Vol. 2, No. 1, 1984, p. 9.
8. Zarqa's classification is adopted; op. cit. See also M. Sebai, op. cit., who mentioned *29* elements of distribution in Islam.
9. For more details on the economic consequences of Islam, particularly divorce, endowments, and egalitarian distribution, see R. J. A. Wilson, "The Economic Consequences of the Islamic Revival," *Contemporary Review*, Vol. 236, No. 1372,1980, pp. 240-245.
10. Cited in M. A. Zaki Badawi, *The Muslim World and the Future Economic Order,* Islamic Council of Europe, London, 1979, p. 113.
11. Mustafa al-Sebai, *Ishttrakiyat al-Islam [Islamic Socialism]*, 1960, p. 200.
12. Yusuf al-Qardawi, *Zaka Jurisprudence* [in Arabic], Part I, Muassaset al-Resalah, Kuwait, 1981 p. 66.
13. A. W. Lewis, *Development Planning,* George Allen and Unwin, London, 1966, p. 123, cited in A. A. Salama "Fiscal Analysis of Zakat with Special Reference to Saudi Arabia's Experience in Zakat," in M. Ariff, Ed., *Monetary and Fiscal Economics in Islam,* CRIE, 1982, p. 343.
14. The term is borrowed from Frederick L. Pryor, *The Origin of the Economy*, Academic Press, New York, 1977, p. 34.
15. "A Contribution to the Theory of Islamic Behaviour in an Islamic Economy," in Khurshid Ahmed, Ed., *Studies in Islamic Economics*, p. 33.
16. "Monetary, Social and International Economics," in *Economics,* Vol. 28, 1983, p. 85. It is true that zakat may not have an immediate, direct effect on growth but it surely does on mobilization (see points 1and 2 above).
17. Narrated by Omar, see M ben Ashur, *The Objectives of Islamic Shariah*, Tunisian Distribution Company, Tunis, 1978, p. 175.

18. A. Zarqa, "Role of Zakat in the Microeconomics and Monetary Policy," Proceedings of the First Zakat Conference, Kuwait, April 30 to May 2, 1984, pp. 273-297.

19. Narrated by Laith from Tawes; see Abu Yusuf, *Al Kharaj,* Industrial Bank of Kuwait (IBK), Dar Al-Shuruk, Kuwait, 1985, pp. 179-186

20. M. Abuzahra, op. cit., p. 486.

21. Abu Yusuf Al Qadi (judge), *Al Kharaj* (The Tax), IBK, op. cit., p. 180.

22. See Abu Zahra, op. cit., p. 486.

23. Narrated by Bukhari and Muslim in Mishkat Al-Masabih, p. 656. Also narrated by Said ibn Waqas in Imam al-Baghawi (436-516 h), *Shar'h al-Sunna, [Explaining Sunna]*, Vol. V, 1-Maqtab al-Islami, Cairo, 1391 (1971), p. 283.

24. See M. Shaltout, *Islam Akidaton wa Shari'a [Islam, a Conviction and a Sharia]*, Dar-al-Shuruk, Beirut, 1983, pp. 244-245.

25. John E. Mandville, "Usurious Piety: the Cash Wakf Controversy in the Ottoman Empire" Items 10 (1979) pp.289,308 cited in Mohammad M Arna'ut, Cash Wakf in Jerusalem during the Ottoman Rule, *Awqaf Journal, Kuwait* No. 9, November 2005. p35

CHAPTER 6

The Islamic State and Economic Intervention

T his chapter aims to demonstrate the role of the Islamic state in the market place as a precondition for shaping the framework of the economic affairs of Islamic society. Essentially, the philosophical implications of this role are significant and include moral, political, economic, and social guidelines. However, it is imperative to note that the dimension and intensity of intervention are dependent upon the degree of growth and development and on both the availability of resources and the equitability of their distribution in a country. Effectively, an underdeveloped Islamic country would experience more intensive state interventions than a more advanced one.

The Scope of Intervention

In essence, the religious teachings from 1) the Quran, 2) the Sunna (ahadith and traditions of the Prophet), and 3) the interpretations of Islamic scholars (*ulamah*) provide the basis for the scope of economic intervention. In this respect, the issue is more straightforward than in Western or socialist systems. In Western economies, only "in the century before Adam Smith [did] political economics set out a considerably wider range of economic policy objectives to be attained by direct government regulations, or manipulation of economic processes."[1] In Islam such rules were established long before.

Smoghi assumed that "laissez-faire, which in Europe did not become an economic theory in practice until the eighteenth century, had been Islamic theory and practice as early as the seventh century."[2] As such, Smoghi's statement supports the argument that the fundamentals of Islamic economic theory were established a long time ago.

By contrast, at its extreme, economic resources in the socialist system belong to the state, leaving no doubt as to the type and scope of economic intervention. As for Islam, the scope of economic intervention is broad and can include state interference in many aspects of economic activity, ranging from guidance and control to the securing of all functions that fulfill society's needs[3]. The following analysis aims to explain and remove the ambiguity attached to such a general statement.

The fundamental duties bestowed in an Islamic state can consist of 1) commanding and obedience, 2) counseling and consultation, and 3) controlling and protecting.

Commanding and Obedience

The commanding function is found in the Quran and it orders the people to obey their Lord, Prophet, and rulers: "Obey God and obey the Apostle and those in authority from among you" (4:59). However, the power of the state or its legislative body is not unlimited. In this respect, the government is bound to intervene and command within the boundaries of Shari'a principles or injunctions. For instance, "the government cannot legalize usury, allow cheating, or disregard the inheritance law."[4] Hence, the government's power of authority is restricted in substance and is not absolute in magnitude. This is a direct application of Quran verse 4:59, which states (i.e., in terms of priority) that God is to be obeyed first, then the Prophet, and, finally, the rulers (represented by the government). This injunction reveals many aspects of the nature of obedience in Islam. The message is perfectly clear and implies that whatever God and His Prophet have ordained to be adhered to literally, and whatever has been ruled by the representative government is to be followed if it is in compliance with the teachings of God and His Prophet.

The Prophet said, "No obedience is due to him who does not obey God."[5] this conclusion stems from the fact that God is the creator, the Apostle is the vicegerent and the ruler is the Apostle's vicegerent, or caliph. Abu Bakr, the first caliph, said in his inaugural speech, "obey me as long as I observe (obey) God and His messenger, (otherwise) you (the people] are not obliged to follow my command."[6] The Prophet's hadith states that[7]

"He who obeys me, obeys God, and he who disobeys me, disobeys God. And he who obeys the amir, obeys me, and he who disobeys the amir, disobeys me. Behold the leader [al-imam] is but a shield from behind which the people fight and by which they protect themselves."

In addition, Islam is against a totalitarian, undemocratic government. The Islamic view of the democratic process differs in substance and structure from the democratic Western system. For instance, in Western democracies the national assembly (or parliament) is free to legislate by a majority vote any laws that seem to be consistent with public opinion. In Islamic law, however, any legislation must be in conformity with the Divine Law. Thus the freedom of expression, though sacred in Islamic law, is bound by the guiding principles of Shari'a, the reason being simple and logical: The Divine Law is more justified, more merciful, and farther from injustice than any man made laws.

Counseling and Consultation

The consulting function is part of the duties of the caliph, duties vested by God and demanded by the community. Consultative traditions in political and communal affairs are the focal point in any democracy. In Islamic democracy it is also a divine duty and a moral obligation ordained upon the ruler and the ruled. In this respect, the Prophet "always consulted his companions as a duty incumbent upon him in his capacity as a Governor."[8] Thus, the duties of the head of state and his ministers are not confined to conducting the state's political affairs but also include guiding the community in all worldly and religious affairs.

This practice was carried out by the Prophet and the caliphs in obedience with the words of the Quran: "Take counsel with them in all communal business [amr] and when you have decided on a course of action; place your trust in God" (3:159).

Interference in the Market Mechanism

In an Islamic economic system the rules of supply and demand are the governing factors that determine prices in the producer and consumer markets. Buyers and sellers can act freely in their commercial transactions without government intervention, except in exceptional cases. These cases are not intended to restrict the freedom of trade; on the contrary, their objectives are mainly to secure perfect information in the market place and to regulate and organize economic activities to protect economic freedom without causing harm or injustice to the buyers or sellers. For instance the Prophet revealed that it is unlawful to go out and meet travelers, sellers, or farmers approaching the city and persuade them that the demand for their goods is small, thus inducing them to sell cheaply. If such a trick is played on anyone, the seller has an option to repudiate the sale after arriving in the market,[9] irrespective of any contract. Thus, the Islamic economy gives due consideration to the elimination of market imperfections.

The modern-day interpretation of the Prophet's message is that it is essential to bring about perfect market conditions in which everybody is informed and aware of prices, as well as the nature of supply and demand. Another message that can be inferred is related to market forces: It is not sufficient to assume perfect information; the authorities must ensure that buyers and sellers are well informed by excluding those who take advantage of the sellers' ignorance and intentionally give false information to induce poor merchants to sell at lower than prevailing market prices.

Price Fixing

Islamic views on government intervention to fix market prices are based on the Prophet's hadith and tradition, which are plainly against price fixing if normal conditions prevail. It has been reported that the people of Al-Madina once told the Prophet, "O Apostle of Allah! Prices of things have risen, price them for us." The Prophet replied, "Allah is the Provider, and [He] who [fixes the] prices, and I hope to meet Allah without being asked by any one of you for an inequality in blood or mal [literally money][10].

Jurists' explanation is that prices increased at the time of this hadith, either due to scarcity or population growth while sellers were pricing their products according to the common practice and norms, without injustice on their part. In this regard, compelling people to sell at predetermined prices is not warranted or justified.[11]

The forces of supply and demand in the pricing structure in Islam are important. Ibn Khaldun recognized the interrelation between supply and demand and the cost of goods. According to him and many "other" Islamic philosophers, including Gazali and Shatibi, human needs and commodities in particular are of three kinds[12]: necessities, conveniences, and luxuries with prices determined by the "cost of labor, duties, taxes and other expenses and from the demand side by the size and intensity of desire of the city dwellers."[13] Ibn Khaldun went on to say that price is affected by the scarcity of goods: "When goods are few and rare their prices go up,"

Islamic scholars have "condemned practices that might disturb the free play of supply and demand."[14] and when goods are found in abundance, prices decline"[15]. As Robinson (1978) rightly points out, the Prophet's tradition has prohibited price fixing and Islamic teachings with respect to commercial transactions are directed toward both sellers and buyers. The latter are induced to give fair prices in bargaining rather than trying to downgrade the goods they are about to buy in order to compel the seller to sell at a bargain price. In the words of the Quran, "Give full measure and full weight, in justice, and wrong not people in respect of their goods" (11:85). On the other hand, motivated by its Islamic duties to protect the public interest, the government may intervene in the market to restore fair competition and prevent monopoly or oligopoly. On monopoly, the Prophet said, "One who provides food is favored with plentiful bounties, but he who monopolizes is accursed and disobedient."[16] However, jurists have differed on whether all commodities are subject to the same injunction against monopoly or whether the prohibition applies to foodstuff only. Abu Yusuf, however, held the view that hoarding anything whose availability is considered of vital importance to society, including gold or clothes, is absolutely forbidden[17]

Economic rationing in Islam should not be taken as a rule but, rather, as a guideline to be applied in emergencies and under circumstances necessitating such action. For example, during the rule of Caliph Omar, rationing was applied to certain commodities (e.g., meat) and a moratorium on planting certain crops in favor of other produce of vital importance was imposed. The rationale was to economize the consumption of a scarce commodity and secure the supply of another during famine or abnormal circumstances.

The superiority of market forces is applied not only to the final produce, but also to factor markets. The level of wages is determined in the labor market according to the rules of supply and demand.

This principle is justified on the basis of freedom of choice and disposition, which are protected in the Islamic dichotomy, naturally, without neglecting the fundamental boundaries of Shari'a principles and limitations. However, there may be cases where government interference in the labor market is considered necessary.

Ibn Taymi'ah held the view that an Islamic ruler may guide citizens toward working in certain professions such as agriculture, construction, and weaving if a chronic need arises. In such cases, Ibn T aymi'ah postulated that workers must be remunerated according to fair market rates at the time. Many other jurists, such as Shafi'i, ibn Hanbal, Gazali, and Ibn al-Jury, share the same views on the ground that weaving, construction, and cultivation are vital industries in any society and, as such, the government is responsible for securing the provision of these services for the betterment of society.[18] On this subject, the late Rector of Azhar, Sheikh Mahmud Shaltut, said, [19]

> This is why the jurists of Islam have stated that it is a religious obligatory duty for Muslims to try to provide for anything that is deemed indispensable to a happy life. If the whole nation neglects the observance of such duties, this means that the whole nation has sinned and they will not be forgiven until these duties are performed by various groups of people each in his particular field.

Therefore, it is the duty of the Islamic state to supervise the job market to prevent unfair competition or exploitation of any kind by enacting the necessary legislation to determine wage policies and contractual relationships among other matters.

Ibn Khaldun advocated a free enterprise system and opposed government intervention in the market. The government's purchase of goods for trading purposes creates 1) unfair competition in the market, 2) a state monopoly, and 3) an escalation in prices so that the government realizes abnormal profits. Ibn Khaldun explained, this leads to 1) putting small traders and workers out of business and 2) killing peoples' incentive to establish or expand their own businesses. The outcome is lower taxes and government revenues until the government finally realizes that the deterioration in revenue outweighs the small benefits obtained from trade. Consequently, diminishing returns and the lack of adequate funds to pay for the army deprive the state of adequate defenses and can eventually lead to its defeat "if attacked by the enemy." Rosenthal commented, "Here is a North African thinker advanced through his own experience in his own land

and in Muslim Spain, a complete theory of human civilization and culture progressing in a politically organized society."[20]

Though this conclusion may be limited to Ibn Khaldun's own time, as Rosenthal pointed out, what is more significance in Ibn Khaldun's analysis is "the causal interdependence of economy, finance and political power, to the exclusion of chance and personal initiative."[1] Notably, Ibn Khaldun's views are shared by many Western and Islamic scholars today who support governments being involved in trade and commerce, with the prospect of raising prices, which is but an indirect tax on consumption.

Al-Hisba (Supervision of Markets)

Having discussed the principles of state intervention in the market, we examine the method by which the Islamic state supervises or organizes economic activities. In earlier times such supervision and organization were carried out by the caliph in person. As the Muslim population increased and the boundaries of the Islamic state expanded, the caliph entrusted the performance of such duties to officers of sound reputation and good faith. The office of the Hisba (censorship) was conducted by *AlMuhtaseb* who was entrusted with the duties of enforcing laws (*ma'ruf*) and preventing illegality (*munkar*). In Islamic law, *ma'ruf* means "any act, word or intention which is good according to the Shara" and *munkar* is "an act, word or intention which is bad according to Shari'a."[21] Thus, the powers, authorities, and duties of the *muhtasib* were so broad that they embodied all worldly and religious affairs. *Muhtasib* duties in the market place encompassed supervisory and deterrent powers. The *muhtasib* must observe all commercial activities, particularly to exert necessary measures in such transactions involving deception, damage, risk, or uncertainty. Technically, this means business transactions that expose a party to excessive risk or damage as a result of uncertainty about the price, quality, or quantity of the product's counter value, the delivery date, and the ability of either the buyer or seller to fulfill his commitment, as well as ambiguity in the terms of the deal, invalid sales, usury, hoarding, monopoly, invalid hires, invalid partnerships, and purchases by payment in advance. The *muhtasib*'s other duties involved enforcing the law in connection with the debasing of currencies, cheating, fraud, theft, involving specific workers and craftsmen such as: makers and weavers, brokers, criers and dyers, cotton spinners, tailors, money changers, phlebotomists and suppers, physicians, oculists, surgeons, bore setters, and instructors of boys, and so forth.

Al Muhtaseb should posses certain attributes to be eligible for conducting his duties. These include: loyalty, firmness, piety, purity, wisdom (incorporating justice, patience and intelligence), kindness and tolerance.[22]

Summary and Conclusion

There have been wide disagreements among Islamic scholars, particularly economists, as to whether Islamic economic teachings favor a market economy, a command economy, or mixed economy. The preceding underlines the limitations and restrictions surrounding Islamic policy toward market intervention. It is established that the need for occasional intervention is necessary to protect the public interest and prevent monopolies. Does this mean that economic freedom, particularly individual freedom, is restricted or violated? The answer to this question may differ from one person to another simply because economists differ in their definitions of individual and economic freedoms. However, the crux of the matter hinges upon the motives behind Islamic government policies. The motives an Islamic government's economic policy are neither 1) to compete in the market or cancel the roles of sellers and producers as separate entities, as is the case in communist economies, nor 2) to fix prices on the ground that sellers and producers are "greedy capitalists" and should therefore be punished. On the contrary, the motives of the Islamic state are realized from the spirit of the Prophet's sayings, which are clearly demonstrated in the treatment of deceptive brokers, who are prevented from exploiting the ignorance of sellers. Thus, the need for regulation and protection arises. Moreover, fair play in the market is protected but monopoly is prevented. Religion, public interests, and private interests are well guarded. However, in the case of conflict, the former is favored. Imam Shatibi pointed out that "in Islam the interests of religion are absolutely higher than the interest of the worldly life."[23]

In Islam, ownership of wealth belongs to God and man is a trustee who is required to follow the precepts and commandments of Allah, the ultimate owner. These teachings call for *Ad'l* and *Ehsan* (justice and benevolence): "God commands justice, the doing of good" (16:90). Individuals and enterprises are expected to serve the public good without neglecting their own interest. While absolute equality cannot be attained, since people differ in their qualities and aptitudes, equal opportunities for those capable of work must be maintained, as well as a minimum subsistence level for the poor and disabled. The driving force behind these principles is social justice, which discourages the concentration of wealth and tries to minimize social differences by applying a system of fair distribution. Among this system's most powerful tools are zakat, awkaf, and the inheritance law (p.10).

The role of the Islamic state is to maintain a balance between private and public interests. This can be achieved by regulating rather than directly intervening in the economic system It is incumbent on an Islamic government to exercise guidance, control, and protection in accordance with Islamic precepts. Private ownership is sacred and there is no limitation to the scope of ownership, provided the owner pays the religious tax and fulfills his or her obligations to God and the community. Economic activities in Islam are well guarded and economic agents are free to conduct their own businesses. The individual is free to choose his work profession, although this freedom is occasionally restricted as mentioned previously (p. 35).

Endnotes:

1. T. W. Hutchinson, *Positive Economics and Policy Objectives*, Allen and Unwin, London, 1964, p. 129.

2. Joseph Smoghi, "State Intervention and Trade in Classical Arabic Literature," *Studies in Islam*, Vol. 4, No., 2, 1967, pp. 61-65. I do not entirely agree that laissez faire was the policy of the Islamic economic order (for reasons outlined herein.

3. See Ibn Taymiah, "al-Hisba fi' Islam", al-Madina: al-Maktaba alElmiah, n.d., pp. 16-19, cited in Mohammed A Saqr, al-Iktisad al-Islami, First International Conference in Islamic Economics International Centre for Research in Islamic Economics, Jeddah, 1980, p. 59.

4. Mohammad Baqir Al-Sadr, *Iktisaduna*, op. cit., 13th ed., p. 30

5. Ahmed Ibn Hanbal, on the authority of Mu'adh ibn Jabal.

6. See Mohammad ibn Jarir al-Tabari, *Tafsir al-Tabari*, Cairo, 1953.

7. Reported by Al-Bukhari wa Muslim on the authority of Abu Hurayrah and quoted by M. Asad in his authoritative and thought-provoking book *State and Government in Islam*, 1980, p. 59.

8. Sheikh M. Abu Zahra, "Human Society under the Aegis of Islam," Academy of Islamic Research Proceedings, op. cit., 1966, pp. 470-471.

9. See Ibn al-Ukhuwan, *The Maalim al-Qurba fi Ahkam al-Hisba*, Reuben Levy, Ed., Cambridge University Press, London, 1938, p. 22. See also Ahmed ibn Taymiah, *Al-Hisba in Islam*, Maktabet Dar al-Bayan, Damascus, 1387 h.

10. See Al-Baihaqi, Ahmed b Husein, *Al-Sunnan al Kubru*, Vol. II, Dar al Fikr', Beirut, n.d.p. 29.

11. Ibn Taymiah, in M. Saqr, op. cit., pp. 58-60.

12. Abdul Rahman ibn Khaldun, "The Prices in the Cities," *Al-Muqaddimah*, Dar al-Kitab al-Lubnani, Beirut, 1979.

13. F. Robinson, *Islam and Capitalism* (Brian Pearce, Trans.) University of Texas Press, Austin, 1928, p. 51.

14. Ibn Khaldun, *the Muqaddimah*, Vol. II, F. Rosenthal (Trans.), Pantheon Books, New York, 1958, pp. 277-278.

15. Ibid, p. 388. See also Abdul Rahman Ibn Khaldun, *Kitab al Ebar*, op. cit., pp. 499-501.

16. Narrated by Abu Dawud al Tirmidhi. See M. A. Al-Jammal, *Mawsuat al Iqtisad al Islami* [*Encyclopedia of Islamic Economics*], Dar al-Kitab, Beirut, 1980, p. 206.

17. See Mannan, op. cit., p. 95. See also Al-Jammal, ibid, p. 206.

18. See Mohammad al-Mubarak, "Tadakhul al-Dawleh al-Iktisadi fi Islam," Proceedings of the first International Conference on Islamic Economy, op. cit., pp. 14-16. See also M. Saq'r, footnotes 2 and 3, pp. 60-61.

19. See Mohamed A. Al-Arabi, "Investment of Capital in Islam," Proceedings of the Second Conference of the AIR, Cairo, 1985, pp. 103-121.

20. For more details, see "Ibn Khaldun," *Bulletin of the John Reynolds Library*, Vol. 24, by E.L. R, 1940, pp. 318

21. Ibn al-Ukhuwan, op. cit., p. 5, *Shara* means the same as Shari'a, that is, legally binding precedents.

22. Abdulmajid B. Muaz, "al Awkaf wa alMuhtaseb", Awkaf journal No 2, Kuwait May 2002, pp.48-54

23. Imam Abu Ishaq al-Shatibi, *Al-Muwafiqat fi Usul al-Sharia*, Vol. 2, 2nd ed., Al Maktaba at Tijariyah al-Kubra, Cairo, 1975.

CHAPTER 7

Money In The Islamic Economy

U nderstanding the concepts of money and riba in Islam is a prerequisite not only to shed light on the nature, methodology, and functions of an Islamic bank, but also to grasp the workings of the Islamic economy at large. We begin this chapter by focusing on money in the Islamic economy

This section examines the origins, nature, and characteristics of currency in the early days of Islam. It also discusses the role of money and its functions, with examples drawn from the early Islamic literature. A brief analysis of the demand for money in the Western economy follows and the Islamic views regarding the motives for holding money are outlined. Due consideration is given to the factors affecting money demand that have not yet received adequate attention in the Islamic literature, including an elucidation of some of the Prophet's ahadith about wealth and money in the context of their impact upon utility and consumption. Islamic views on bartering as well as hoarding is also discussed.

The Development of Islamic Currency

The currencies in circulation during the first two decades of Islam were the Byzantine dinar (gold) and the Persian dirham (silver). These remained in circulation until the 18th year of Hijra denoted by the letter *h*), when Caliph Omar minted a replica of the Persian dirhams, adding the words *Messenger of God* on a square shape coin. The first Islamic dinar was minted during the reign of Abdel Malek ibn Marwan (76 h), during the Omayyad dynasty.[1] Consequently, the use of the Byzantine dinar was prohibited except when re-struck as indigenous tender. The sayings of the Prophet and the interpretations of the early Islamic scholars in the following passages relate directly to gold and silver currencies. Ever since paper currency was first introduced in the 16th century, Islamic contemporary jurists have argued that as long as paper currency fulfills the same functions as a metal currency, particularly as a medium for pricing goods and services, it must be subject to the same rules and injunctions.[2]

The Meaning and Nature of Islamic Money

In Arabic *mal* or *al-mal* means money. According to Ibn al-Atheer (d. 606 h), *al-mal*, used to stand for gold and silver and only later meant all types of wealth (literally *al-Tharwa*[3]). Thus the terms for money and wealth are used interchangeably in the Islamic literature. However, Islamic jurists have classified *al-mal*, or wealth, into monetary (*Nuqu'd*) and non-monetary assets (*Arud*) and capital (*Ras'mal*). This distinction is important and helps clarify the meanings of the Quranic verses and the Prophet's *ahadith*, whenever the term *money* or *wealth* is used. The purpose of this section is to focus on the demand for money in the Islamic economy. Thus, the term *money*, unless otherwise indicated, will reflect the same meaning as used in Western economies. It is widely accepted by Islamic and Western economists and historians that evolution from a barter economy to a commodity economy and then to a monetary economy happened gradually. Initially several commodities, including precious metals, were used as a medium of exchange. Through elimination, precious metalsgold and silver emerged as an acceptable means of pricing all other products. Abu'l Fad'l al-Dimashqi (570 h) related the invention of money to the need for "creating a medium of exchange to ease the problems associated with barter". His thoughts were almost identical with authors of contemporary economics. He even mentioned the need for labor specialization and the coincidence of wants, concluding that the "necessity for a standard of value as a medium for pricing things" was accentuated by the following factors[4]:

a. People's need and dependence on each other.
b. The desires of one person do not necessarily coincide with those of another.
c. The quantities ofNeed are not equal.
d. The determination of exchange rates between one product and many others is difficult

Al-Dimashqi attributed society's preference for and acceptance of gold and silver to these metals' malleability, durability, attractiveness, divisibility, and difficulty to counterfeit.

Money in the Quran and the Sunna

The Quran mentions *al-mal* many times and describes it as an allurement, a gift, and a bounty of God, as revealed in the following verses. "Wealth and sons are allurements of the life of this world (18:46)" Offspring and wealth (including money) are objects of comfort, delight, and pleasure (*mata'*): Beautiful for mankind is love of joys [that come] from women and offspring and stored heaps of gold and silver, and horses branded [with their marks], and cattle and land. That is comfort of the life of the world. Allah with him is a more excellent abode." (3:14)

Yet, if money is a bounty and a gift, it must not be mishandled or used to inflict injustice or injury upon others. To circumvent such incidents, the ownership and dispersion of *mal* is governed by Shari'a principles, which forbid usury, hoarding, and extravagance: "You do not really possess of your wealth but that you eat and use up, that you dress and wear up, and that you spend on charity and preserve for the afterlife."[5] In the first part of this hadith the Prophet emphasizes that the demand for money is a matter of choice among different assets. Real possession is not the material holding of wealth (including money), since possession without utility is useless, like a mirror that reflects no object. Hence goods are held or possessed for the real satisfaction they provide to the holder through the ability to consume to the point of depletion, exhaustion, or deterioration. Optimal utility is reached, according to the Prophet, when one gets the best out of goods and services or uses them to the utmost.

According to M. Kahf, the relation between real income and consumption was defined by the Prophet to equal the "total of what is used for the purchase of goods and services that produce immediate satisfaction in the life plus that which is given away for causes that enrich one's afterlife."[6] Most likely Kahf meant true income or material income by *real income;* this term should not to be confused with real income adjusted for inflation.

In the second part of this hadith, satisfaction is not confined to consumption for immediate needs or for enjoyment in this world but extends far beyond. In an Islamic context, charitable individuals are rewarded in the afterlife. The third major meaning that can be inferred from this hadith is that real utility from an Islamic perspective is attained through 1) consumption in this world and spending for the afterlife (charity) and 2) rational spending. In the case of wasteful spending and extravagance, full consumption, that is, optimal utility, is not reached; satisfaction is constrained by the individual's absorptive capacity and declining marginal utility. The Prophet asked his followers, "For whom among you is the *mal* of his heirs dearer than his own *mal*? They answered, "Everyone sees *his* mal dearer than his heirs. And then the Prophet said, "Your *mal* is what you use up and your heirs *mal* is what you leave."[7]

The message of this saying consists of the following:

1. Money is precious among Muslims and the Prophet acknowledges this fact.
2. The people feel that their own *mal* is dearer to them than that of their heirs, though in the final analysis their money eventually passes into the hands of their heirs.
3. The paradox of the previous item is explained by the fact that the enjoyment of wealth is bound by the individual's absorptive capacity, although it could be argued that, mathematically, an extra earning of one pound will lead to more satisfaction than the previous pound. It is also true that the desire for money can be infinite and one's wealth countless; however, at a certain level the individual's' absorptive capacity and the law of declining marginal utility dictate that the $(n + 1)$ unit of a good will not provide any more satisfaction than the nth unit.

The Characteristics of Money

Money is thought to be characterized by the following properties that allow it to achieve its proper role in the economy: scarcity, liquidity, stability, circulation, and neutrality[8]. Both Islamic and Western economists agree on the properties of scarcity, liquidity, and stability. Although all systems recognize the importance of money circulation, Islamic teachings, through moral persuasion and ordinances, have regulated and organized the use of money at the individual level. In Western economies, monetary control has reached an advanced stage of sophistication at the macro level. It should be emphasized that the elements of comparison between Islamic and Western economies are lacking. For instance, there is a time barrier between Islamic views on money and contemporary Western theories. Therefore, our aim is to expound the Islamic views with respect to money and how these would affect the demand for money in today's world rather than compare the two systems.

Scarcity

Scarcity is determined by the fact that if money were in abundance, it would be worthless and useless as a means of payment, since nobody would be willing to accept it in exchange for goods and services. As Imam Gazali (1058-1111) said, "among the bounties of Allah are the creation of the dirham and dinar . . . [they are] scarce in themselves and they are not objects of desire."[9] The fact that money is desirable means it is scarce.

Liquidity

Liquidity is the benefit emanating from accepting money as a means of payment. Thus, liquidity means that money can be exchanged directly for goods and services, at any time, without resorting to other media. In this regard, Gazali states, "Who possesses them [gold and silver] possesses everything."[10]

Stability

Islamic jurists emphasize stability in the value of money (see Ibn Khaldun below) and even regard this quality a priori reasoning for accepting a currency as legal tender. Magrizi (801 h) wrote about price stability and inflation and called for the reservation of gold and silver as a standard of value.[11] In Western economies monetary stability has become one of the main goals of economic policies. Although the purchasing power of money fluctuates with changes in general price levels, its value is stabler than that of many different commodities. Nevertheless, its nominal value has remained constant.

Circulation

The importance of money circulation in the economy can be inferred from certain deeds, injunctions, and reported tradition, including 1) the banning of bartering in five main commodities, 2) the imposition of zakat (religious tax) on income and wealth, including idle bank balances, 3) the degrading of hoarding, and, finally, 4) the stress upon growth, development, and investment of all types of wealth, including money. All these topics are discussed in chapter 9: demand for money. At this juncture it is worth noting that it was common practice before and during the early days of Islam to rent agricultural land in exchange for food or similar non-monetary items. However, the Prophet banned this practice, allowing only the use of gold and silver as means of payment. Regardless of the main causes of this ruling, which might well have been to preserve justice and eliminate disputes, our intention here is focused on its monetary implications. Undoubtedly, this rule leads to enhancing the process of monetization and increases the turnover of money in the economy.

Concerning the ruling by Hanafi jurists on the necessity of using commercial dirham as capital in commenda (*mudaraba*), Udovitch commented,[12]

> This is more than an example of the responsiveness of Hanafi law to encompass needs and realities. From an economic point of view it indicated that commerce had at its disposal the entire reservoir of monetary resources of the Medieval Islamic world.

> This not only facilitated the financing of trade, but could also stimulate its velocity by making available all kinds of currency in an age when the supply of standard, good quality coins was not always adequate.

The Role of Money in Islam

The basic functions of money in today's world, excluding the implications of interest, are identical in both Western and Islamic economies. These functions include the use of money as a medium of exchange or a means of payment, a standard unit of measurement, and a store of value. Islamic jurists and economists have emphasized the role of money as a medium of exchange, regarding this correctly as one of the main reasons for the invention of money. Gazali said,[13]

> Allah created dinar and dirhams as judges and intermediaries among other types of al Amwal [wealth] which can be estimated among them thus their creation is meant to circulate among people and serve as intermediary among al Amwal. The other wisdom is to use them as a means to acquire other objects.

The role of money as a standard measure of value or a unit of account eliminated the problems inherent in determining the exact exchange rates between different types of products. Money serves as a common denominator for pricing all types of goods and services. However, its use as a unit of account differs from country to country and depends largely on the degree of bankability in an economy, since current and deposit accounts are widely used as units of account.

Ibn Khaldun (1332-1406 AD) noted that money is not only used as a medium of exchange but also acts as a store of value by virtue of its function as a means for deferred payment and as a saving medium[14]:

> God created the two mineral "stones," gold and silver, as the [measure of] value for all capital accumulations. [Gold and silver are what] the inhabitants of the world, in most cases, consider treasure and property. Even if, under certain circumstances, other things are acquired, it is only for ultimately obtaining [gold or silver:
>
> All other things are subject to market fluctuations, from which gold and silver are exempt. They are the basis of profit, property and treasure.

Finally, for these functions to be fulfilled, acceptability and recognition, either by law or common practice, is a necessary condition for any currency to act as legal tender.

Endnotes:

1. Ibn Khaldoun, cited in Rafic" al Masri "al-Islam wa'Nuqud" [Islam and Money], discussion paper, CRIE, 1981, p. 76.
   e. People's need and dependence on each other.
   f. The desires of one person do not necessarily coincide with those of another.
2. See, for instance, the resolutions of the Council of Islamic Jurisprudence Makkah, 8-16 rabi' II, 1402 h.
3. See M. H. Makhlouf, Tabyan fi Zakat Al-Athman [Explanation of zakat on currency] Cairo, 1344 h, p. 23.
4. *Al-Ishara ila Mahasen al-Tijara* a reference to the advantages of trade], M. Ashour, Ed., Dar al-Itihad al Arabi l' Tibaah, Cairo, 1973, quoted by A. O. Metwali and S. I. Shehatah, *Economics of Money in the Islamic Thinking* (in Arabic), Maktebet Wahbeh, Cairo, 1983, p. 39.
   g. The quantities ofNeed are not equal.
   h. The determination of exchange rates between one product and many others is difficult
5. Narrated by Imam Muslim; see Imam Al-Nawawi, (d. 676), Riyad al-Saleheen, Isa al-Babi al-Halabi, Cairo, n.d., p. 221.
6. See "A Contribution to the Theory of Consumer Behaviour Society," in Kh. Ahmed, Ed., op. cit, p. 23.
7. Narrated by al-Bukhari; see Imam al Nawawi, Riyadh al-Saleheen, op. cit., p. 249.
8. Ihya'Alum al-Din, Kitab al-Shukr, cited in R. al-Masri, 1977, p. 177.
9. Ibid.
10. Ibid.
11. Magrizi (766/1364-845/1441), cited in Rafic al-Masri, "al-Islam wa Nuqud," op. cit., 1981, p. 68. Maqrizi is a 15th-century historian who wrote many books (e.g., *Shazuz al-uqud fi zikr' Nuqud* [*Treatise on Money*] and (*Ighasat al Umah Bikashf al-Ghuma*) about the history and causes of starvation in Egypt and the impact of inflation on prices.
12. Udovitch A. L., *Partnership and Profit in Medieval Islam*, 1970, Princeton University Press, Princeton, p. 180.
13. Ihya' Alum al-Din, op. cit.; see also El-Gousi, 1982, p. 167.
14. Ibn Khaldun, Rosenthal (Trans.), op. cit, p. 313, with minor modifications by the author.

CHAPTER 8

The Demand for Money in Western Economies

The analysis of demand for money has passed through three major phases of development in Western economies. The first phase began with Ricardo and other economists who argued that in the long run the stock of money is proportionate to price. This approach was stressed by Irving Fisher (1867-1947), who emphasized the relation between money and economic activity, or, as Laidler put it, "the transactional velocity of circulation" in an economy.[1] Fisher argued that the quantity of money times its velocity of circulation will equal the number of transactions undertaken times the average price level.[2] Hence, by introducing the velocity concept, Fisher concluded that the price level is proportionate to the money supply in the long run.[3] This relation is expressed in terms of the identity equation

$$MV = PT$$

Where M is the amount of money in circulation, V is the velocity of exchange, P is the average price level, and T is the volume of transactions

Laidler commented that while Fisher was concerned with the factors that determine the amount of money in an economy, the Cambridge School economists' approach was concerned with the individual's demand for money. This brings us to the second phase. Instead of asking what amount of money is needed to carry out the transactions in the economy, as Fisher did, the Cambridge economists were concerned with how much money an

individual "wants" to hold. The demand equation for money as introduced
by Marshall and Pigou[4] is

$$M_d = KPY$$

In this equation the demand for money is a function of income for
each individual and ultimately for the aggregate economy. This conclusion
implies, as Hosek argued, that the demand for money in the short run is
insensitive to changes in interest rates and the velocity of money is constant.[5]
On the other hand, Laidler remarked that the Cambridge school did not
ignore the effect of income, wealth, and interest rates for holding money.
Rather, it failed to study the relation between these variables and their
individual impact on the quantity of money and emphasized the stability of
the relation between income and the demand for money.

The third phase came about with Keynes, who emphasized the
motives underlying the demand for money.[6] He identified three motives:
transactionary, precautionary, and speculative. The transaction motive,
or liquidity preference, is derived from the use of money as a medium of
exchange. People want to hold money to acquire goods and services in the
ordinary course of business. In addition, the precautionary motive dictates
the need to meet unexpected obligations and contingencies. This motive
is reflected by the necessity of keeping a certain amount of money in idle
balance. However, there is an opportunity cost associated with retaining an
idle balance reflected in the yield or interest rate forgone by not putting the
money to use.

Keynes stressed the importance of the rate of interest and bond prices
in determining the demand for money. In his view the demand for money
depends upon peoples' expectations of future trends in interest rates and
bond prices. If, for instance, an individual (or firm) expects interest rates to
rise in the future, he would want to hold money in interest-bearing deposit
accounts. He might also liquidate his bond portfolio, if he has one, to avoid
a capital loss. Provided all wealth holders behave similarly, this behavior
contributes to an increase in the demand for money balances.

On the other hand, if the interest rate is expected to fall, that individual,
according to Keynes, would want to buy bonds since bond prices will
rise. Through a gradual process of changing expectations, wealth holders'
demand for bonds rises, thus contributing to a fall in the demand for money
balances. Tobin and his Yale associates later expanded Keynesian theory by
asserting that interest rates and bonds are not the only determinants of the

demand for money[7]. They developed a portfolio approach that recognized the availability of a wide range of financial and non-financial assets for savers (households and institutions). The rates of return are determined by the possibility of substituting between these assets and the quantities that people would want to hold of each. However, we are not concerned here with the effects of monetary policy on bank credits or the money supply and the reader is referred to Tobin.

Endnotes:

1. See D. E. W. Laidler, *The Demand for Money*, Intertext Books, London, 1969, p. 4.
2. Ibid.
3. R. C. Amacher, *Principles of Macroeconomics*, South-Western Pub. Co., Cincinnati, 1980, pp. 151-154.
4. Laidler, op. cit, pp. 48-49.
5. William Hosek, *Monetary Theory*, Richard Irwin, Homewood Illinois, 1975, p. 165.
6. J. M. Keynes," *The General Theory of Employment, Interest and Money*", Macmillan, London, 1936, pp. 168-170.
7. For more details on the portfolio theory, see James Tobin, "Money, Capital and Other Stores of Value," *American Economic Review Proceedings*, No. 2, 1961, pp. 26-37, op. cit.

CHAPTER 9

The Demand for Money in an Islamic Economy

The motives for holding money balances per se have not garnered adequate coverage in the Islamic literature. While many authors have analyzed the role of money in Islam and discussed directly related subjects, they have not focused on the motives of money demand This chapter aims 1) to discuss whether the traditional motives for holding money are accepted or rejected in the Islamic point of view and 2) to explain the religious factors with the greatest influence on the demand for money.

The factors influencing the demand for money can be grouped into internal and external factors. Internal factors refer to individual preferences and tastes such as social status, level of income, extravagance, and greed. External factors refer to ethical, religious, and governmental influences through legislation and regulation. In this respect, any ethical and religious influences that may have a major impact on Muslims behavior in the holding of money are discussed in this chapter. Fiscal influences such as taxation and government regulations are not discussed, they are beyond the scope of this study.

Generally, the demand for money in Western and Islamic systems arises from a need to carry out transactions and to meet contingencies. The transaction and precautionary motives arise from the role of money as a means of payment. Thus, holding money in the Islamic economy is justified by the need to settle debts (most frequently by checks, e., money) and to meet dayto day expenses. Any analysis of the demand for money in the Islamic economy must take into consideration the banning of interest. Thus, speculation regarding changes in interest rates and their impact on bond prices in the Keynesian dichotomy, or any interest-motivating behavior, has no role in the demand for Islamic money.

Profit is seen as the substitute for interest in the Islamic economy and as such will be the criterion for the allocation of resources in the private sector. to establish profits as the sole yardstick for the allocation of resources, savers can attach a premium to their profit expectations to cover against business risks (e.g., competition, product saturation) and inflation. In other words, investment decisions in an Islamic economy must account for a host of factors, including profit anticipation.

Since Islam has no restrictions against investments, trading in financial and physical assets is permissible. Thus, in the Islamic system a saver/ investor can choose a combination of investment outlets, ranging from Islamic Sukuk (Islamic bonds) to real estate. It is imperative to point out, however, that in the absence of interest the speculative demand for money and financial assets will be less apparent than in the conventional system. Some Islamic economists even postulate an increase in the demand for real assets in a riba-free economy. Their argument is based on the assumption that these assets are a suitable substitute for money balances. Zarqa asserted that since there is no apparent evidence in Islam against using money as a store of value, the demand for money would be influenced by the rate of "halal" return and the degree of risk of other assets (financial or real). This influence, the author continues, is compatible with the economic argument that was clearly defined in the portfolio balance approach outlined by Tobin and his Yale associates.[1]

However, it is worth mentioning that holding money is not without cost. In the Islamic economy, as mentioned earlier, the cost of holding money helps in keeping down the demand for money balances. This cost is higher in Islamic than in conventional economies. It includes zakat payment at 2.5% on money balances, plus the opportunity cost, as well as custodian charges. In addition, the speculative demand for money is minimized by the prohibition of interest and the imposition of zakat on wealth, including idle balances. According to Chapra, this reduces "the locking-in effect" of interest rates and secures greater stability in the total demand for money.[2] However, in an Islamic economy, speculation may decrease but it would not entirely disappear. Moreover, the impact of zakat will not be as great since it is imposed on articles of trade at the same rate as on money balances.

What would happen if profitability declined below a sustainable level? A sensible answer is that savers would hold money balances to the point at which the current net benefit of holding money is greater than the net present value of investment. That is, the asset demand for holding money would decline in the face of rising trends in idle money balances.

Factors Affecting the Islamic Demand for Money

Islam bitterly condemns money hoarding. God threatens those who hold money and abstain from spending in the way of Allah with severe punishment:

> They who hoard up gold and silver and spend it not in the way of Allah, unto them give tidings (O Muhammad) of a painful doom, on the day when it will (all) be heated in the fire of hell, and their foreheads and their flanks and their backs will be branded therewith (and it will be said unto them): here is that which you hoarded for yourselves, now taste of what ye used to hoard. (9:34)

God does not ignore human nature and the lust for wealth and power; many verses the Quran, describe man as selfish, niggardly, and very possessive: "Say if ye had control of the Treasures of the mercy of my lord, Behold, ye would keep them back, for fear of spending them, for man is ever niggardly" (17:100). Hence if hoarding is condemned and mankind is, by nature, likely to be begrudging and stingy, Muslims are urged to develop and invest their wealth on the one hand and economize in their spending and pay generously for charity on the other. The Prophet said, "If anyone revives dead land, it belongs to him, and the unjust root has no right" and "He who has money should develop it; he who has land should cultivate it."[3] Malik explains that "the unjust root is whatever is taken or planted without right." God says, "Make not thy hand tied (like a niggard's) to thy neck, nor stretch it forth to its utmost reach, so that thou become blameworthy and destitute" (17:29).

As a result investment is a moral and religious duty and one of the means against hoarding. However, Islam does not provide a clear definition of hoarding. The *Fuqaha* (Islamic jurists) do not agree on what constitutes hoarding and what does not. Imam al-Qurtubi (d. 671 h) pointed out that Islamic scholars were uncertain whether hoarding applies to money and wealth, even if these have been reduced by zakat (alms tax) payment, or whether it is confined solely to money or wealth on which zakat has not been paid. He also said, "Sharia has approved holding wealth (*dhabt al-mal*) and paying its dues., that is the holder must pay zakat on idle wealth balance. Ultimately the capital wealth will be wiped out by zakat and nobody in this Ummah [nation] decrees that," and gave as an example the wealth of some of the Prophet's companions to support his views.[4]

Ibn Omar, an Islamic jurist, was of the opinion that "hoarding excludes money on which zakat has been paid,"[5] while money is said to be hoarded if zakat has not been paid on it. This opinion coincides with a Prophet's hadith that says, "God did not ordain zakat but to purify what remained [saved] of your money, and ordained inheritance law to leave it [inherit it] to your descendants."[6] This hadith implies that saving is lawful in Islam and to detach wealth from hoarding, it should be "purified" by zakat: "Blessed by God he who earned lawfully, spent willingly, and saved for his poor and needy day."[7] According to this hadith, the Prophet defines savings as the difference between earnings and expenditure and as such it is not hoarding, provided 1) zakat is paid on savings and 2) the intention for saving is precautionary. However, the level of saving, which is by definition a residue, can differ drastically from one person to another, depending on their level of earnings and expenditure.

Hence, it is hard to seperate in monetary terms, between savings and hoarding, simply because individuals are not alike in their spending habits and the expectations of their future needs or incomes differ, even if they share a similar income stream. It is prudent to assume that a rational Muslim individual would keep his money balances to a minimum to avoid erosion of its value via zakat or inflation. Moreover, a rational investor would search for investment channels, motivated by a number of factors, including religious and moral obligations that encourage investment and forbid hoarding and economic factors that dictate the necessity of investment as a hedge against inflation and as a means of wealth accumulation.

The preceding discussion on money and wealth may give the impression that hoarding relates only to monetary or financial assets. In effect, hoarding can encompass all kinds of property when its withholding would harm the public. This view is held by Imam Abu Yousuf, who believed that hoarding applies to any commodity, including gold, silver, clothing, and food. His theory rests on the belief that "he who hoards such commodities abuses his right of ownership since hoarding of cloth is just as harmful as hoarding food" and "the community would suffer from the hoarding and monopoly of food as from the hoarding and monopoly of clothes."[8] He also stressed that suppressing any of the various needs of society is wrong and unjustifiable.

Although the above views have some merits, they may be more applicable under exceptional circumstances, such as famine or war, rather than in periods of normality. It is hard to regard the hoarding of food in normal times as the same as hoarding clothing or vice versa! Indeed, Abu Yusuf's views are not shared by all jurists and Imam Ahmed and al Shafi'i think that the Islamic prohibition of monopoly relates to food products only.[9]

Thus it may be safely assumed that the hoarding of money can exist when someone withholds or retains an idle money balance for a prolonged period, over and above his immediate needs (for transactions and contingencies), with no intention of investing or giving to charity, provided at all times that this sum of money is considered excessive by any standard. Scholars and economists have argued that money should not be lockedup or withdrawn from circulation for fear of the hoarding effects. These effects tend to reduce the supply of money, which, if things remain equal, leads to an increase in the price of goods and services, resulting in a lower demand, a decline in output, and eventually rising unemployment. However, it does not appear that temporarily keeping one's savings in liquid form to benefit, for example, from expected changes in relative prices of assets is haram (unlawful). Besides, the abolition of interest will deprive money of its liquidity premium, eventually leading to the disappearance of the speculative motive for holding cash (which is, currently, largely dependent on the fluctuations of interest rates).

Money and Bartering in Islam

The Prophet explicitly organized barter deals for six vital commodities: gold, silver, dates, barley, wheat, and salt. According to Sunna, bartering in these commodities is mainly subject to two restrictions: First, exchanging or selling homogeneous commodities against themselves with excess profit is not allowed. Second, the transaction must be on a spot basis; that is, exchanging a bar of gold to be delivered immediately for another bar to be delivered in the future is not permissible. Thus, spot deals are lawful whereas forward deals are not (when the exchange is between two similar things).

According to Abu Said al Khudari, [10]

> Bilal brought to the Prophet, peace be upon him, some barni [good quality] dates, whereupon the Prophet asked him where these were from. Bilal replied, "I had some inferior dates which I exchanged for these two sa' [a measure] for a sa'." The Prophet said, "Oh no, this is exactly riba. Do not do so, but when you wish to buy, sell the inferior dates for [cash] and then buy the better dates with the price you receive."

Two reasons were cited for this rule: 1) Replacing money for barter has eliminated the injustice or injury normally associated with the valuation and determination of exchange rates among different products and 2) the belief that bartering can lead to *riba al-fad'l* (literally, excess), which is prohibited. Riba al-fad'l occurs, for example, when someone exchanges one bushel of wheat for one bushel and half to be delivered at a future date.

As far as the demand for money is concerned, the regularization of barter transactions, as explained earlier, facilitates the exchange of goods and services and increases the velocity of the circulation of money. This is due to the intermediation process through money, which was enhanced by the Prophet's command. One would think that these benefits have no modern implication, since monetization is widespread. However, if we consider the amount of barter trade, which has reached about 30% in 2010 of all worldwide export trade, we can only imagine the chilling effect of the regularization of banks on the future of this trade with the Muslim world if the Islamic code were strictly enforced.

Summary

The introduction of money has facilitated exchange transactions and obliterated the problems of bartering. On the other hand, the reverence for money has created problems associated with hoarding and the welfare of the Islamic society. The second major problem associated with the monetary economy is the possibility of creating a contradiction between money as a medium of exchange and money as an earning asset or commodity. While the basic functions of money are accepted and recognized, Islam has regulated and formalized a set of rules and principles to bridge the gap between the supply of and the demand for money through the abolition of interest, hoarding, and, to a lesser extent, speculation. Through zakat, charity, and the inheritance law, wealth, including money, is meant to circulate and change hands. This injunction came in recognition of the fact that only through the mechanism of circulation can the process of economic growth and stability be achieved.

Endnotes:

1. See, for example, A. Zarqa, "The Demand for Money in an Islamic Economy," unpublished paper (in Arabic), November 1984.
2. Omar M.Chapra, *Toward a Just Monetary System,* Islamic Foundation, Leicester, 1985, pp. 187-188.
3. Al Jamch I'Ahkam al-Quran, op. cit., pp. 24-25.
4. Ibid., p. 22.
5. Narrated by Abu Dawoud on the authority of ibn Abbas, ibid., p. 22.
6. Quoted by Metwali and Shehata, op. cit., p. 26.
7. Ibid, p.26
8. M. A. Mannan, *Islamic Economics: Theory and Practice.* Ashraf Publishers, Lahore, 1970, p. 95.
9. See Sayid Sabiq, Figh Al Sunna [*Sunna Jurisprudence*], Vol. 3, Dar al-Kitab al-Arabi, Beirut, n.d., p. 401.
10. Narrated by Muslim. See Sahih Muslim bi Sharh 41 Nawawi, Kitab al-Musaqat, Bab al-ta am mithlan bi mithlin (Book of Irrigation), Vol. XI, al Matba'ah al Misriyyah, Cairo, 1349 h, pp. 13-16. This hadith was quoted earlier but is repeated here because of its importance.

CHAPTER 10

Al-Riba in Islamic Jurisprudence

The most controversial aspects of Islamic economics that set it apart from conventional systems are the prohibition of riba and hoarding and the imposition of zakat. The abolition of riba has economic and social consequences. On one hand, it aims to eliminate injustice (*zulm*) and encourages brotherhood and cooperation between capital and labor by promoting productive enterprises and curbing personal loans for speculative purposes.

Zulm occurs when debt matures while the borrower is insolvent and the lender multiplies the debt for no reason other than delayed payment; on the other hand, it aims to

Generally, all financial and commercial transactions, with few exceptions, are permitted in Islam, provided certain rules and obligations are observed. On the other hand, so called riba (usurious) deals are absolutely forbidden in Islam. The first part of this chapter defines the literal meaning of riba. The second part discusses the types, boundaries, and scope of riba. Finally, an outline of some early and contemporary Islamic thought on the reasons for banning riba are presented. This will serve as a guide to Islamic economics, which is the major focus of this book.

The Meaning of Riba (Usury)

The word *riba* in its ordinary usage before Islam was different from its meaning in Islamic law. Initially, in Arabic, *riba* literally meant an increase and an addition (*ziyada'*), an excess, an augmentation, or growth (*Nama'*). The verb *raba* (to increase) signifies a certain augmentation over an original value or status. In Islamic law riba signifies an addition obtained in an unlawful manner. This unlawful addition could be implicit or explicit, as in a sale, a loan, or virtually any contractual agreement. An illegal contract is said to have a condition bearing an excess accruing to one party with no consideration given to the other. Ibn Jarir al-Tabari (d. 310 h), a Quranic commentator, said,[1] "A creditor is called Murbi (one who augments) because he doubles the amount of the debt." However, not everything that increases (*yarbu*) is usury or unlawful. For instance, profits from trade and mark-ups on sales are legitimate and lawful. In addition, the verb *rabat* (to grow) is used in the Quran in a positive manner: "Thou seest the earth barren and lifeless, but when we pour down rain on it, it is stirred to life, it swells, and it puts forth every kind of beautiful growth (in pairs)" (22:5).

Types of Riba

According to Ibn Rushd, scholars agree that al-Riba is mainly found in 1) selling, that is, selling forward the six basic commodities for the same genre (e.g., one bushel of wheat in exchange for one bushel and a half to be delivered at a future date), and 2) liabilities arising from a sale, a credit (*salaf*) or any other transaction.[2] He also mentioned that scholars' opinions varied on whether repaying a debt before maturity for a discount is riba or not. In the view of Sheikh R. Rida, is not riba since the latter implies an increase, whereas the discount is a decrease in liability for early settlement.[3] Riba in exchanging the basic six commodities is widely known as riba alQard'l (excess) or riba al-biyuh (sale), while riba in one's liability is known as riba al-Jahili, or riba in debt (see below).

Debts, Loans, and Mortgages

In Islamic law, debts originate from various transactions, such as deferred sales, rent payments, unpaid dowries and loans. Contemporary use the word *debt* for a loan and vice versa. Consequently 1) riba in debts originating from a deferred sale is sometimes confused with 2) sales riba, which can result from exchanging gold, silver, and vital food items, the sale of which were regularized by the Prophet. The first is called riba al-Nasia' and the second is called riba al-fad'l.

In a debt contract the debtor becomes liable to the creditor for the debt. The debt must be in writing, payable on the due date, and no excess is allowed over the contracted sum if payment is rescheduled.

The Quran lays down the rules and conditions pertaining to the contractual agreement between the debtor and creditor: "When you deal with each other in contracting a debt for a fixed time, write it down and the one who owes the debt dictate" (2:282). "If you are upon a journey and you do not find a scribe then a security may be taken into possession" (2:283). To acknowledge the wisdom and significance of these verses, one should realize that the majority of the addressees were illiterates at the time of the revelation. The emphasis on writing contracts and calling witnesses not only seek to establish law and order to minimize disputes and eliminate injustice, but it also shows the importance of writing and reading and encourages literacy.

A loan (*qard*) is said to be confined to tangible things (*Mithliyyat*) and must be payable in its own genre. Under Islamic law a loan is a benevolent act and the lender should not stipulate a benefit from the borrower or seek material reward. God says, "Who is he that will loan to God a [benevolent] loan, which God will double unto his credit and multiply many times? It is God that grivet (you) want or plenty, and to him shall be your return" (2:245). Giving a benevolent loan is thus commendable (*Mandub*) by Shari'a.[4] This analysis shows a legal difference between a debt and a loan that has no economic consequences.

Mortgages are allowed in debts, including loans. The mortgagee is allowed to use the mortgaged property in compensation for expenses incurred in maintaining the mortgaged assets (e.g., a house). Since lending and borrowing are inevitable on mortgages, the Prophet said,[5]

> The mortgaged animal may be used for riding, when it is
> mortgaged, on account of what is spent on it, and the milk of
> a milked animal may be drunk when it is mortgaged, and the
> expenditure shall be borne by him who rides [the animal]and
> drinks [the milk].

"The Prophet once bought food from a Jew on credit and he mortgaged an iron shield."[6] Jurists agree that the mortgagor is permitted to use the mortgaged asset if the mortgagee gives prior consent,[7] but if the consent was a precondition in the mortgage contract, the mortgagee is not allowed to use the mortgaged asset to avoid riba.

Quranic Injunctions against Riba

In recognition of human nature and the influence of customs and belief on one's conduct, riba was gradually prohibited in Islam by revealing at first the fundamental principles of the forthcoming duties of Muslims and what might involve unlawful deeds. In the beginning, the Quranic verses compared riba and zakat, expressing God's discontent with riba and His blessing for zakat donors: "That which you give in usury in order that it may increase on (other) peoples' property hath no increase with Allah: but that which ye give in charity, seeking Allah's countenance, hath increase manifold" (3:39).

Recalling that in the first fase the Quran draws a comparison between zakat and riba, in the second phase regarding Quranic injunctions against riba, the intention was to preach and warn by revealing to Muslims the destiny of those who disobeyed God's teachings in the past and how they were liable for severe punishment: "That they took usury, though they were forbidden; and that they devoured men's substance wrongfully; we have prepared for those among them who reject faith a grievous punishment" (4:160).

In the third phase the verses were more specific and decisive and left no doubt that doubled or multiplied riba was no longer allowed: "O ye who believe devour not riba [usury], doubled and multiplied: but fear Allah; that ye may [really] prosper. Fear the Fire, which is prepared for those who reject faith" (3:130-1) It has been acknowledged that the following verses about riba in Surat al-Baqara were among the last ordinances by God and that the Prophet died before he was able to explain them to his companions:

> Those who devour riba will not stand except as stands one whom the Evil one by his touch hath driven to madness. That is because they say "sale is like riba" but God has permitted sale and forbidden riba. Those who, after receiving direction from their Lord, desist, shall be pardoned for the past; their case is for God (to judge), but those who repeat (the offense) are companions of the Fire: they will abide therein (forever). God will deprive riba of all blessing, but will give increase for deeds of charity: for He loveth not creatures ungrateful and wicked. O ye who believe fear God, and give up what remains of your demand for usury, if you are indeed believers. If ye do it not, take notice of war from God and His Apostle. But if ye turn back, ye shall have your capital sums: deal not unjustly, and ye shall not be dealt with unjustly. (2:275-9)

The apparent meaning of these verses signifies that a sale, unlike riba, is a legitimate act. It follows that profits from sales are also lawful and acceptable. The profits, if any, are but an increase over the cost of a sale and this increase is not forbidden on the premise that trade is lawful. All Muslim scholars agree that sales are permitted to facilitate the exchange of benefits in the community. This exchange would not have taken place if profits were not allowed. Otherwise, there would be no inducement for sellers to exert some effort to cater to the needs of society without undue hindrance. Ibn Jarir said, "The increment [profit] that results from trade differs from that which results from delaying the due date . . . Allah says, I have forbidden the latter and permitted the former."[8]

Pagan Arabs did not differentiate between riba where the return is almost guaranteed and sale where profits are not certain.[9] the determination of the scope, including the meaning of unlawful riba as mentioned in the Quran, may hinge upon identifying the meanings and kinds of usurious transactions that were common in Arabia during the Quranic revelation, since most probably these same usurious practices are those condemned and forbidden by the Quran. Unfortunately, the Prophet's companions, Quranic commentators, and Islamic scholars (*Fuqaha*) differ not only on this issue but also on whether the term *riba* mentioned in the Quran is collective or general.

The jurists confirm that for a term to be collective, its literal meaning should differ from its juristic meaning (which was unknown before the revelation). Examples of such terms are *zakat* and *salat*, whose literal meanings are growth and to call upon God, respectively. For a term to be general, it must have one meaning and no need to be explained by the Sunna. Jurists who believe that *riba* is a collective term assume that not every increase is riba (e.g., profits in a sale). Those who believe that *riba* is general assume that only the riba that was familiar during the revelation is that which is prohibited by the Quran.[10]

Basically the Islamic *Fuqaha* unanimously agree that the *riba* mentioned in the Quran relates to riba al-Nasia (deferred usury). For this reason, the *riba* in the Quran is commonly referred to in jurisprudence books as riba al-Nasia or al-Nasa'. It is also widely accepted that riba al-Nasia' is essentially found in debt transactions and for this reason the *riba* mentioned in the Quran is sometimes referred to as riba in debts (riba al-duyun) and, again, riba jahillya. It should be emphasized, however, that while the majority of the Islamic schools agree that the Quranic prohibition of riba is indisputable, they may differ on certain matters (see the controversy on riba al fad'l p.70).

In analyzing the riba in debt, we ought to know first whether the debt is initiated from a sale, a loan, or some other transaction. Second, what sort of "addition" is haram? Is it the first addition at the time of the debt contract or the second and subsequent additions on or after the first and second due dates?

Third, is the "amount" of deferred debt related to the face value (the initial capital) or other sum(s) involved?

Regarding the first question, Imam Malik stated[11],

> Usury in the Jahilliyah was that a man would give a loan to a man for a set term. When the term was due, he would say, "Will you pay it off or increase [in the amount due to] me?" If the man paid he took it, if not, he increased [his debt] and lengthened the term for him.

This simply means that at time t_o a sum of dm100 was due creditor C (see the table below). At time $t + 1$ (the due date), debtor D failed to pay. Consequently the original debt (Po) was doubled to 200, to be repaid at time $t + 2$, as shown in the following table.

Po	dm100	dm200	dm300
	Payment	payment	payment
t_o	$t + 1$	$t + 2$	$t + 3$

So far one can conclude that the original debt (Po) is unknown, because Malik said the loan was due, which means Po must be either equal" or less than 100 (Po ≤ 100). However, the example tells us is that the riba "Range" is located between $t + 1$ and $t + 3$, provided the debt was settled between points $t + 1$ and $t + 3$. Yet this conclusion is by no means decisive (see al-Jassass and types of loans p.). Describing riba in pre-Islam, Qutada stated, "Riba al-Jahilly is selling on credit for a specified period. Should the debtor be insolvent at the due date, the creditor increases [the debt] and grants him [the debtor] respite.[12]

Evidently, the riba described by Qutada consisted of deferred debts. These debts were obligations initiated in sales transactions. Another type of sale, also common pre-Islam, involved credits that were repaid in kind. Imam al-Razi explained this transaction by saying that a debtor (a farmer) who presumably owed a whole year's worth of harvest to a creditor would retain one-half of the crop, giving the second half to the creditor, undertaking at the same time to deliver double the quantity in the year that followed. In*Ahkam al-Quran*, al Jassas (d. 370 h) stated,[13]

> Al-Riba which was known and practiced by the Arabs, was the lending of al darahim [plural of *dirham*] and al dananir [plural of *dinar*] for a specified period of time in consideration for an agreeable increase [to the parties concerned]. This was known and common practice among them in those days. It is a well known fact that riba al-Jahilliyah was a deferred loan with a conditional increase added to it. And this increase is in exchange for an extension.

The preceding passages answer the second question since they demonstrate the origins of debt in the pre-Islamic period and lead us to believe that the riba mentioned in the Quran most probably includes riba in sales and in loans. This is evident in the commentary of al-Jassas, who explained that riba in Jahilliyah was the stipulated increase at the time of the contract, and from Ibn Qutada, who pointed out that riba in sale occurs when debt matures and is then increased or deferred.

The following attempts to determine the scope of the forbidden riba.

The Scope of Riba

The determination of the forbidden riba in sales and loans is linked with whether riba arises at the time of the debt contract or at the time of the rescheduling. In this respect we must differentiate between two cases: sales contracts and loan contracts.

In a sales contract, it is apparent that the margin on sale is lawful and thus the amount of debt in one's obligation includes the sales price (cost of sales plus seller's profits), which could be called capital. Thus, when the Quran says, "You shall have your capital sum" (3:279), it means that the seller is eligible to recover the sales price, that is, his capital. The debtor is obliged to pay the debt in full, as agreed upon. On the other hand, the creditor is not allowed to augment the sales price on the due date in case the debtor defaults and should not receive any compensation for postponement. In *Mujmah al-Sayan*, Abu Jaafar b.Ah Al-Tabarsi (d. 561 h) explained the meaning of the Quranic verse in Surat al-Bakara: "sale is like usury" is attributed to the pagans, who used to say that sale without riba is like sale with riba. He quoted Ibn Abbas,[14]

> The man among them used to say when his debt falls due and his creditor demanded payment: "Grant me time and I will increase you in *al-mal* [literally money]" . . . when they were told this is riba, they reply both are the same, indicating that the excess in price at the time of sale, or the excess thereto at maturity due to the postponement are alike. God had threatened and condemned them because of this, and condemned their acts in saying, "And God has permitted sale and forbidden riba." That is God has permitted trade that bears no riba and has forbidden that which bears riba.

The difference between the two is that in one the excess is to defer debt and in the other a lawful profit is attributed to a sale. In addition, a sale involves an exchange of one thing for another, that is, the price is in exchange "for the priced," while al-Riba is an excess without exchange, with only the due date being delayed or the genre increased.

Given the above evidence, it seems rather puzzling why so many Islamic scholars hold the view that riba al-Nasia' is not confined to the increments incurred after the first and subsequent due dates but includes any additions stipulated at the time of the debt contract. These views are discussed shortly. Nevertheless, it has been established that riba al-Nasia or riba al-jahilli can never be at the time of sale in fair trading activity for the reasons mentioned (for similar reasoning, see Ibn Jarir al-Tabari[15]).

Types of Loans

It has been established also that riba al-Nasia' may originate from a loan transaction as well as from a sale. By applying the same methodology, it can be safely assumed that loans in pagan Arabia were of different kinds, including benevolent loans (*qurud hasana'*) and loans with stipulated increases attached to them.

Benevolent loan obviously have no additions to the face value of the loan, whether in money or in kind. The borrower is expected to return the borrowed sum, or anything borrowed, for that matter, without an increase or decrease. This loan can be for a specified or unspecified amount of time, depending on the will of the parties concerned. However, a benevolent loan can be regarded as a gift or alms if the donor so declares at or after the borrowing date.[16] Thus, in cases where maturity dates are not declared, the lender must wait until the borrower is able to repay the debt or revert to customs and traditions. However, if the maturity date is known, the debtor is inclined to honor his obligation on the due date. If the borrower is insolvent, the lender has no option other than to grant him respite. Under Shari'a, a benevolent loan is payable on demand, but the lender is always asked to wait if the borrower is insolvent "If he is insolvent grant him respite" (2:280), since it is absolutely unfair and unlawful to increase the debt after the due date, in compliance with the general rule cited earlier for riba al-Nasia. Moreover, a benevolent loan is, by definition and by nature, an interest-free loan and God urges Muslims to waive their rights if the debtor faces extenuating circumstances.

Undoubtedly the majority of loans in pagan Arabia were usurious, as revealed from historical events transmitted to us. Ibn Hajar al Haithami (d. 974 h) stated,[17]

Interestingly, this description falls within the boundaries of the riba in the Quran, as if the Quranic ordinances in Surat al-Baqarat address this particular practice. For instance, when God says, "O ye who believe fear Allah and give up what remains of your demand for usury," mean that the creditor in the aforesaid example is ordered to relinquish his alleged right to the increments after the due date and can recapture his capital sum, God says, "But if you repent your capital is yours." However, is it only by chance that the loaned capital in this example is the same term (i.e., capital) as used by the Quran. Or is it not? In other words, are the monthly payments that were paid regularly by the debtor, which are almost identical to the interest payments on a bank loan, forbidden riba or not? There is a consensus among Islamic scholars that the forbidden riba referred to in the Quran or Sunna is the riba stipulated in a loan contract and initiated from the postponement of debts, as mentioned earlier.[18]

Riba Al-Fad'l

Riba al-fad'l is the excess received for exchanging two commodities of the same kind. riba al-fad'l is found in three cases: in a sale, in a barter trade, and in an exchange transaction.

Riba in Sales

Buying a commodity (excluding gold and silver) for cash or on credit is permissible. Al-Bukhari reported A'ishah (the Prophet's wife) as saying, "The Apostle of God, peace is on him bought food from a Jew for a deferred payment and he mortgaged for it a coat of mail made of iron."[19.] The permissibility of buying or selling on credit is approved by the majority of Islamic jurists. They have also allowed profit in cash sales to differ from credit sales.[20] In other words; the scholars have allowed an increase in the price of credit sales in lieu of the postponement.[21]

It is forbidden to sell one of the basic commodities (wheat, barley, dates, and salt) for either gold or silver for future delivery. The spot sale of these commodities for gold or silver is permitted at the spot prices prevailing at the time the deal struck. The Prophet said, "If these classes differ [the six classes above], then sell as you wish if hand to hand."[22]

Riba in Bartering

In principle, bartering a commodity for another class of commodity is allowed on two conditions:

1. If the two commodities are among the four basic items (e.g., wheat for dates), the exchange is permissible if their quantities are not equal, providedthe delivery takes place instantaneously.
2. If only one commodity among those exchanged belongs to the four basic items or neither is, there is no restriction on the quantity or time of delivery. The Prophet said, "Dates for dates, wheat for wheat, barley for barley, salt for salt, like for like, hand to hand, he who increased or delayed [delivery] committed Riba except of different classes" (narrated by Abu Hurairah).[23]

The Prophet banned the bartering of one sa'a (a type of measurement) of certain kinds of dates for two Sa'a of lower-grade dates and ordered to sell and buy for cash. The Prophet once said the following to a man who used to do just that:[24]

> Do you take one Sa' for two? He replied, "Messenger of Allah!
> Why should they sell me good dates for assorted low quality

dates, Sa'a for Sa'a!" The Messenger of Allah, may Allah bless
and grant him peace, said, "Sell the assorted ones for dirhams,
and then buy the good ones with those dirhams."

Riba in bartering and lending also occurs when one of the four basic
commodities is either spot or forward exchanged for different weights of
the same commodity, because it is difficult to assess the exact value of the
exchanged items without the intermediation of money. To prevent injustice,
the Prophet permitted the spot exchange of equal quantities of these
commodities.

Riba in Exchanges (Sarf)

This section discusses exchanging gold for gold, silver for silver, and gold
for silver. Buying gold for gold is permissible if the transaction is concluded
instantaneously and the weights are equal.

The same rule applies to silver. Equality in weight is not required in
exchanging gold (dinar) for silver (dirham), since their genres are not equivalent
The rate of exchange must be the spot rate at the time of the contract with
immediate delivery (i.e., reciprocal exchanging of the two currencies).

The Prophets ahadith pertaining to riba al-Sarf are as follows:

> "Let dinar be exchanged for dinar with no addition on either
> side or dirham be exchanged for dirham with no addition on
> either side."[25]

> "Gold for silver is usury except hand to hand."[26]

Omar ibn al-Khattab reporting Allah's Messenger, Ibn al-Khattab,
said, commenting on this hadith: "If someone asks you to wait to be paid
until he has goneback to his house [to bring the money], do not leave lest
it be considered as adebt or something deferred. For that reason, Imam
Malik said this transaction isdisapproved of and the "exchange collapses if
settlement is delayed.

> "There is no harm in taking [dinars and dirhams] at the
> current rate so long as you do not depart leaving something to
> be settled."[27]

The Controversy

The controversy surrounding riba al-fad'l is the reconciliation of two views: one restricting riba al-fad'l to those cases where the exchange, barter, or sale of the same commodity or currency involves forward delivery and the second controversy involves the scope of riba al-fad'l. The proponents of the first view depend on hadith Usama ben zey'd, which the Prophet said, "There is no riba except in al Nasi'ah and "No riba in what is traded hand to hand.[28]

Though the majority of jurists do not question the authenticity of these ahadith, they give various interpretations. Al-Sarakhsi (483 h), for example, commented,

Probably the narrator (Usama) heard the Prophet answering a question on al-Riba in such types, as gold for silver, and dates for wheat, saying 'Verily al-Riba is found in 'al Nasi'ah however he might not have heard the question.[29]

The second controversy involves the scope of riba al-fad'l, that is, whether it is confined to the six commodities or includes other items as well. The majority of the Islamic jurists of the various schools hold the view that riba al-fad'l, though applicable to the famous six commodities (gold, silver, wheat, barley, dates, and salt), encompasses all other commodities that interact with the aforesaid six with the same causation (illat) that leads to riba al-fadl, though jurists differ widely on the causation or attributes that permit this analogy.

1   The juristic reasoning of the Zahiri School excludes analogy According to this school, riba only pertains to gold and silver and does not apply to other currency, save paper money, nor to commodities other than those mentioned by the Prophet. The Shafi'i School has asserted that the riba ordinances govern all edible commodities, including such items that are countable and can be sold as individual items. The Maliki School has ruled that the riba ordinances include every edible commodity sold by way of a scale or that could be stocked like corn and rice. Said al-Musayyab said, there is usury only in gold or silver or what is weighed or measured of what is eaten or drunk.[30]

The Hanbali School and a number of independent scholars have envisaged that bartering any two commodities of the same genre and quality should be governed by the Prophets injunction. An example of this is steel and textiles. The opinion of the Hanafis depends on the Prophet's hadith narrated by Obada ibn al-Samit: What is weighed is like for like if it is of the same genre, if the two kinds differ there is no harm [i.e., exchanges of different weights are valid]."[31]

Note that the six commodities subject to riba al-fad'l have the following properties:

1. They are used as either money (gold and silver) or as quasi-money.
2. Some of them are sold by weight and some by measure.
3. Four of them were used as an essential food item at the time of the ban.

It follows that inclusion of an additional commodity, either by analogy (qiyas) or reasoning (ijtihad), should be subject to the following conditions:

1. There should be a genuine need to do so, as in the scarcity of the item(s).
2. It should be used as either money or quasi-money, taking into consideration that the paper currency presently differs from gold and silver by chronic fluctuations and erosion in purchasing power.
3. Any attempt to include new items at present should not be made if the said commodity is not classified as essential. Reference should be henceforth made to the four original items at the time of the prohibition of riba al-fad'l.

The driving force in deciding whether a new food product falls within the same category of the famous four items should be governed by the fundamental principle in jurisprudence that says., Freedom of action in the'field of mundane transactions is the rule.'[32] Thus, it would be prudent to assume that if the Prophet wanted to incorporate other commodities in the ban, he would have said so. On the contrary, he said that If the classification differs from the six commodities you can sell as you wish (riba in bartering p.89). On the other hand, any attempt to include items not listed by the Prophet should be restrictive and not absolute. Any unlisted commodity that could be listed under the banner of riba al-fadl should possess at least all the properties of the four commodities together and not only one of them, [33]

1. The alleged commodity is classified as an essential food item.
2. The alleged commodity is sold by measure or weight.

4. The alleged commodity is used or could be used as quasi-money, especially if it is used in exchanging other food items.
5. The alleged commodity should be as nutritious as wheat and corn and as vital as salt, belong to the cereal group, and have the ability to be stored without fear of decay

This is only a proposition prompted by the fact that the Prophet, according to all authoritative reporters, forbade the six items in His ahadith and mentioned no other items. The arguments among the Islamic schools of thought on this issue have not produced any convincing opinions. For this reason, many Muslims have been inclined to accept the Zahiri views, even though they do not accept the Zahiri stance, because the Zahiria do not believe in analogy in fiqh (jurisprudence). In their opinion, fruits and vegetables should be excluded because the Prophet does not mention them.[34]

Certain trends were advocated by minorities: The first expresses their stand toward fixed rate profit in cash waqf. It was customary since the eighth century of Hijra during the Ottoman rule to set aside an amount of money as cash waqf to be lent at a fixed rate (10-11%). Some of these transactions were sanctioned by Imam Zufar in 158 h (see the Waqf p. 36). It was alleged, on the other hand, that providing cash on a *mudaraba* basis is subject to the risk of the donor (*rab al-mal*) losing the waqf capital. This was justified on the basis of necessity to preserve the emphasis on money through risk-free investment at that time (1932).

The second trend believes that interest is forbidden on consumption loans. The famous scholar politician Maarouf al-Dawalibi concluded that the banning of interest applies to consumption loans alone, and not to productive ones.

The third approves of fixed interest on banks' deposits and bonds. This trend was advocated by the late mufti of Egypt Sheikh Sayed Tantawi who also declared that fixed interest on bonds and bank deposits are not haram on the ground that these are contemporary transactions that do not resemble any practice during the Prophet's time.

The Shari'a stands on these allegations are in order.

> "Riba is practiced when a man gives his money to someone else on credit, on condition that he [the creditor] takes from him [the debtor] every month a specified sum and the capital remains intact. On the due date the man claims his capital, if the debtor defaults he increases in the right and in the

duration. This is called Nasia" [postponement], though it also applies to riba al-fadl [excess] because the purpose of this is the deferment'. **Economic Considerations for Prohibiting Riba**

This section first summarizes the wisdom of prohibiting riba and, second discusses the wisdom of prohibiting riba al-fad'l. In banning riba, Islam seeks to establish a society based on justice and brotherhood. The Quran says: But if ye turn back, ye shall have your capital sums: deal not unjustly and ye shall not be dealt with unjustly (2:279). Additionally, Al-Mawdudi mentioned that injustice associated with riba leads to moral, social, spiritual, and economic harm.[35] According to Islam, earnings and profits should be commensurate with work effort. Lending money for interest permits a lender to augment his capital without effort, since money does not create a surplus value by itself. Only through the marriage of labor and capital can a surplus or deficit occur. Thus, it is fairer for a provider of capital to share the profit or loss with the entrepreneur than to obtain a fixed return (regardless of the outcome of the borrowers business).

An Islamic injunction against riba addresses all kinds of consumption or productive loans. At the time Islam recognizes that people's need for money is not confined to productive purposes, since there are needs such as consumption and emergencies. Though some consumption loans can be obtained on an interest-free basis, the Islamic state is responsible for fulfilling many of these needs through an elaborate system of distribution (see Chapter 1) and through moral teachings to enhance the spirit of cooperation, brotherhood, and spending in the way of Allah.

Notably, almost all the verses of the Quran that mention usury are either preceded or followed by verses urging people to give charity and zakat, as in this verse: That which you give in usury in order that it may increase on [others] people's property has no increase with Allah: but that you give in charity, seeking Allah's countenance, has increased manifold (3:39).

Banning riba also aims to eliminate the exploitation of the needy and to prevent selfishness, which is normally associated with lending.

In promoting the spirit of cooperation and caring, the Islamic state guarantees the repayment of debts on behalf of debtors. The Prophet says, Whoever leaves property, it is for his heirs, and whoever leaves a burden, it shall be our charge.[36] Historic and modern scholars alike agree that the riba system 1) deprives society of capital needed for productive investment and 2) prevents capital owners from engaging in productive enterprises that require labor and hardship, as long as return on capital is easily obtained through lending. In contrast, Claude Henin points out those interest-free loans contribute a good deal to the economic growth of the country and the dissemination of wealth by allowing poor and middle class individuals to get funds under exceedingly favourable conditions.[37]

Islam has therefore forbidden riba in all its forms and types. In this respect there is no difference between a consumption loan and a productive one; individual loans and loans from or to the government are all banned.

Why Riba Al-Fadl Is Banned

The *first* broader justification for banning riba al-fadl in gold and silver can be inferred from the initial sayings of the Prophet. When asked about the wisdom, he replied, I fear Rama, [riba] for you.[38] The *second* wisdom is to give just measure and full weight, by eliminating means of deception. The *third* justification is to not monopolize scarce food in expectation of future profit.

On the other hand, the ban of the sale of gold for gold unless for the same weight happened at a time when various kinds of coins were exchanging hands. The debasing of currency was widely practiced and thus, to protect the ignorant from deception and fraud, it was necessary to establish certain measures to introduce well-defined criteria. As such, there was an insistence upon weight more than on numbers in exchanging gold and silver. Malik stated[39]

> According to the way things are done among us there is no harm in selling gold for gold and silver for silver by counterpoising weight, even if 11 dinars are taken for 10 dinars hand to hand, when the weight of gold is equal, coin for coin, even if the number is different. Dirhams in such a situation are treated the same way as dinars.

Abu Zahra emphasized that the banning of riba al-fadl was aimed at establishing a perfect measure of value.[40] This is why the Prophet ordered the intermediation of money and restricted and regularized bartering when exchanging two commodities, whether of the same or different kinds. Thus, when a buyer sells his poor-quality dates and buys with the proceeds high-quality dates, justice and fair trading prevail, whereas in a strict barter deal the exact worth of each class would not be known and hence one of the parties would be deceived.

Ibn al-Qayyim, an Islamic jurist, spoke about the wisdom of banning riba al-fad'l and cited more than one justification, including the prevention of a monopoly on food: to keep prices down and to avoid deferred riba.[41] A monopoly on food would be avoided by banning the sale of the main food provisions for future delivery and by disallowing disparity in bartering for commodities of the same kind. Thus, if no one is allowed to make a profit in deferred trading, one would want to sell a commodity promptly, before it perishes. Food would thus not become scarce and the needy would have two options: either buys at the market price or resort to barter trade.

The banning of riba al-Fad'l has eliminated the injustice and injury associated with the difficulty in determining a fair measure of value and, more significantly, has closed the backdoor to riba al-Nasia (deferred riba), in accordance with a Shari'a rule that states that anything that serves as a means to the unlawful is also unlawful.[42]

Endnotes:

1. In Jameh al-Bayan, quoted in Rashid Rida, *Al-Riba wal Mu' amalat fi'l Islam,* B. Bitar, Ed., Maktabet al Qahira, Cairo, 1960, p. 61.
2. Muhammad Ibn Rushd (Averroes), *Bidayet al-Mujtahed wa Nihayat al-Muqtased (The Beginning and the End),* Part 2, 3rd ed., Mustafa al Bahi. Shalabi and Sons Library and Press, Cairo, 1960, p. 128. Also Rida, Mohammad Rashid, *Tafsir al Manar* (alManar Translation), 4th ed., Maktabat al Qahira, Cairo, 1960.
3. Op. cit., 1960, 70-71.
4. For a brief outline on jurists' opinion on loans, see R. al Masri, "Al-Nizam al Masrafi al Islami," in *Dirassat Fi al-Iqtisad al-Islami,* the Second International Conference on Islamic Economics, CRIE, 1985, pp. 184-185.
5. Narrated by Abu Hurairah, in *Manual of Hadith,* p. 321; see al Shafi'i in *al-Umm,* Vol. 3, IBK, Kuwait: op. cit., pp. 184-186.
6. Narrated by A'ishah in Sahih al Bukhari, Dar Ihya'al Turath al-Arabi, Vol. III, Beirut, n.d., p. 113.
7. See Ali al-Khafif, Ahkam al-Muamalat al Shariah fi al Islam, Cairo, n.d., 1947, p. 119.
8. I. Z. Badawi, *Nazariet al-Riba Muharam Fi Sharia Isl amieh,* Council for Art, Literature and Social Sciences, Cairo, n.d., p. 62.
9. From Rouh al-Ma'ni lil-Allussi (d. 1270 h), \Idaret al Matba'h al Munirieh, Vol. 3, Cairo, n.d., p. 43.
10. See El-Gousi, op. cit., 1982, p. 1559.
11. Related by Malik on the authority of Zayd ben Adam, Alruiwatta, 1982, p. 304.
12. Cited in R. Rida, op. cit., p. 63.
13. Cited in R. Rida, op. cit., p. 63.
14. Quoted by Rida, op. cit., p. 66.
15. Tafsir al-Tabari, al-Tabari, Commentary of Quranic Verses, Vol. II, Dar al Ma'aref, Cairo, n.d., pp. 29 -30.
16. See Ibn Qudama, al-Mughni, Riyadh, Maktabet al Riyadh al-Haditheh, Vol. IV, n.d., pp. 350-360.

Riba is practiced when a man gives his money to someone else on credit, on condition that he [the creditor] takes from him [the debtor] every month a specified sum and the capital remains intact. On the due date the man claims his capital, if the debtor defaults he increases in the right and in the duration. This is called Nasia' [postponement], though it also applies to riba al-fadl [excess] because the purpose of this is the deferment.

17. Ahmed ben M. ben Ali, al-Zawajer an Iqtiraf al Kaba'ir, 1st ed., Vol. II, al-Matba'ah Azharieh, n.d., Cairo, p. 180.
18. The opinions of the majority of Islamic jurists are adopted throughout this book as regards interest or riba, which are both forbidden.
19. See Sahih Muslim, Ministry of Awkaf and Islamic Affairs, *al-Dar al Kuwaitiah L'l Tibaah wa Nashr*, Kuwait, 1969, p. 15.
20. See N. Ott'r, al Muamalat, al-Masrafieh wa Rabawieh wa Elajuha fi Islam, 4th ed., 1980, p. 93. See also R. al-Misri, Majallet al-Umma, Jumada II, 1406 h, pp. 54-59.
21. Imam al Shukani, Nay'i al-Awtar, "Shefa'Galil fi Hok'm Ziyadet al-Thaman Lemujarat al-Ajal" [A treaty on the decision of increasing the price for the sake of delay], Dar al-Jeel.
22. On the authority of Ubadah ibn al-Samit in Sahih Muslim, Kitah al-Buyuh, Hadith No. 3853, p. 834.
23. Quoted by Jamal Attia, "Banking Operations in an Islamic Framework," *Majallet al Muslim al-Muaser*, No. 38, p. 95.
24. Related by Malik in al-Muwatta, p. 288. For the implications of this hadith, see the *Concept of Money in Islam*, above
25. Abu Huraira reporting to Allah's Messenger, in Sahih Muslin Hadith No. 3858, p. 834.
26. Al-Muwatta, p. 292.
27. On the authority of Ibn Oimar, in Sunan Abu Dawud, Vol. 11, pp. 952-953.
28. Reported by Ibn Abbas, quoted by Sami Homoud, 1982, p. 155.
29. M. A. Sarakhsi, Al-Mabsout, Matbaat al-Sadeh, Cairo, 1324 h, p. 112.
30. Al-Muwatta, op. cit., p. 291.
31. Quoted by S. Homoud, 1982, P.161
32. See Attia, op cit, pp. 97-98.
33. For example the hadith narrated by Muslim, cited in M. Hamshari, 1971, p. 192, has forbidden the six items; see also al-Muhalla, Vol. 8, pp. 467-468.
34. Some jurists (e.g., Malik bin Anas) exclude perishable food items. See Al-Mawdudi, *A Riba*, M. Al-Hadad (Trans.), Dar al-Ansar, Cairo, n.d., p. 98.
35. See al-Riba, op cit, pp. 40-62.
36. Narrated by Bukhari, *Manual of Hadith*, Muhammad Ali, Ed., p. 320. Also cited in A. S. al-Masri, op. cit., p. 100.

37. Claude Henin, "Financial Infrastructure of Saudi Arabia," Institute of International Cooperation, University of Ottawa, March, 1980, p. 6,
38. Al-Muwatta, op. cit., p. 291.
39. Al-Muwatta, op. cit., p. 292.
40. Tahrim al-Riba" p. 31, quoted by El-Gousi, op. cit., 1982, p. 166.
41. Ibid., p 169.
42. Cited in Mashal D. Al Mashal, the Kuwait Finance House: Viability of Growth as an Interest-Free Financial Institution, unpublished PhD dissertation, International University, San Diego, 1987, p. 42.

Conclusions to Part I

In *al-Mukaddemah* (literally, introduction), the historian and social scientist Ibn Khaldun (808/1406) scientifically analyzed the causes of the rise and fall of nations. In his first book of seven "al-Ibar" (the maxim) he draws his conclusions by recalling lessons from history (*ibar*) and analyzing the interrelations between moral, psychological, political, economic, social, demographic, and historical factors. He advise the monarch in a concise and eloquent manner:

> The strength of the sovereign (*al-mulk*) is not accomplished except by the implementation of Shari'a. The Shari'a cannot be implemented except through the people (*al-rijal*).
>
> The people cannot be sustained except by wealth (*al-mal*), wealth cannot be acquired except through development (*al-imarah*).
>
> Development cannot be attained except through justice (*al-adl*).
>
> Justice is the criterion (*al-mizan*) by which God will evaluate mankind, and the sovereign is charged with the responsibility of actualizing justice.

The Prophet (PBUH) has been reported to have said the following:

> How can a Governor I have appointed say; this is for you [the treasury] and this is a gift for me? Why does he sits in his parent's home and see if he gets these gifts? By God, in whose hand is Muhammad's life, any one of you who takes [unduly]

anything from thus [what belongs to this treasury] will have it around his neck on the "Day of Judgment."[1] The Prophet then raised his hands and said twice, "O God: Have I conveyed?"

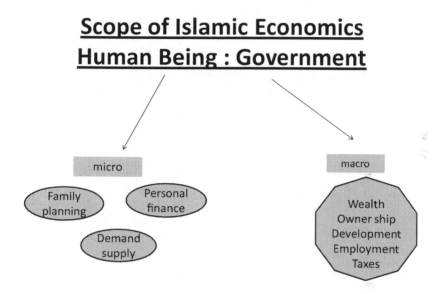

PART II

THE ISLAMIC ALTERNATIVE

CHAPTER 11

Issues, Impediments, and Solutions to Islamic Finance

Deficiencies in the Existing Banking System

The following briefly analyzes the deficiencies in the conventional banking system with respect to the Islamic perspective. These deficiencies in the banking sphere and the Kuwait stock market crash of 1982, led to what came to be known as Al Manakh crisis in Kuwait. The repercussions of Al Manakh crisis, are also examined as it is a reflection of the repercussions in the rest of the Gulf region and many Third World nations as well.

Though the crash happened years ago, it is still a significant case study with lessons to draw from today. First the drawbacks in the conventional system are examined followed by analyzes of the areas violating Shari'a code of conduct.

Injustice and Inequality

The more obvious drawback in the current system relates to the creditor-debtor relationship. In this system loans must be paid on maturity regardless of the outcome of the business for which credit was originally granted.

Disenchantment of Profitable Businesses

Even before the Al Manakh crisis, traditional conventional banks were failing (particularly in Kuwait) to efficiently spread lending throughout productive and non-productive sectors. This is partly due to commercial banks being concerned with collateral rather than with the purpose of the loan or the type of business of the borrower.

Deficiencies in Borrowing Lending Instruments

Apart from issuing shares, potential borrowers have variety of instruments for raising funds. For example, bonds can only be issued by banks and large investment companies. It is widely recognized that banks usually favor large corporations and wealthy businessmen in granting overdrafts and personal and financial loans over smaller entrepreneurs.

Deficiencies in Stock Market-Related Lending

The tendency or preference of conventional commercial banks passive lending, particularly through unsecured personal and financial loans, has encouraged speculation in real estate and the stock market. Worldwide some banks including Islamic banks have even failed to exercise reasonable diligence in financing speculators.

Purchasers of shares in Kuwait were allowed to borrow up to 100% of the value from brokers or finance companies. Additionally, payments were exercised through post-dated checks, which totaled 94 billion among 6000 debtors.

The Kuwaiti stock market collapse which came to be known as Al Manakh crisis also revealed many areas in the financial system that was in violation of the Shari'a code of business ethics, including the following:

- Indulgence in riba at rates far beyond the legal ceiling
- Selling what one does not own or buying what one cannot afford. For example, selling orders were not backed by possession of the stock. Dealers trade from their own account without restrictions on volumes, margins, or prices.

- Committing *gharar* by artificially raising prices. Some top banking officials were able to make 'monopoly' gains for themselves. They bid prices up by creating artificial demand or by fixing the price that reflected their biased desire rather than the expected future return of the share.

With their traditional emphasis on trade and name loans (personal and financial), many banks in Kuwait were not able to react quickly to the changing financial patterns or to the decline in economic activity. Weak control by the supervisory authorities and a lack of strategic planning and long-range forecasts of markets, sectors, and political trends have further exacerbated banking problems.

Overall private sector financing by Kuwaiti commercial banks has been in decline reflecting the downturn in the economy. Above all, this decline has revealed the unwillingness or inability of banks to identify and pursue profitable customers and businesses. Non-conformity with current laws and Islamic business ethics, favoritism in lending, the encouragement of speculative activities, and inappropriate financing methods show that the current financial system is inherently inequitable and inefficient and leads to speculation in financial and real assets. Under these circumstances, the current system must adapt to the future financial requirements examined in the following chapters.

Many other regulations and deeds were violated. For example, some banks lent to their directors prior to shareholder approval, violating international and local charters. Obviously had government been hesitant in offering solutions and committing public funds, the political, social, and economic consequences of the Al-Manakh saga would have been even more devastating. The following were some of the major repercussions of the crisis:

1. Land prices fell far short of dealer expectations. Consequently, the huge capital gains that were expected in the peak years have turned into huge capital losses.
2. The banks' capital base deteriorated and abnormal reserves were depleted in a bid to compensate for doubtful debts. All Kuwaiti banks except for one were on the verge of collapse.
3. Kuwait's financial reputation in the international money and capital markets was badly hurt.
4. Confidence and trust among dealers and traders, deeply cherished in Kuwaiti society, was shaken.

5. Commercial and service firms were forced to close and thousands of workers lost their jobs. In addition, companies that survived the crisis experienced many abnormal cash shortages and were not able to pay their salaried employees.

Many investors' life savings in Kuwait and elsewhere were wiped out or significantly diminished. The Kuwaiti government had to draw on foreign reserves to avoid a collapse of their banking industry and to restore confidence in the system. Consequently, the Kuwait stock market collapse to a massive debt default, known as the debt crisis. A total of 59,064 debtors failed to service their debts, owing KD 4.4 billion to the banking sector at the beginning of 1985. Unserviceable loans represented 40% of the entire sector's financing.

After two years of volatility and turmoil, the government put forward a resolution called the Debt Resettlement Program to solve the debt crisis. Briefly, the rescue package called for the following[2]:

(a) For firms with negative cash flows, the rescheduling of secured and unsecured debts over a 10-year period, net of interest

(b) For defaulters with positive cash flow, payments of 7% interest on non-performing loans over a 15 year period.

(c) The conversion of debt to equity.

(d) The eligibility of debtors' companies for working capital or refinancing facilities, provided these companies are carefully evaluated before granting the loan.

(f) The state's commitment to support bank shareholders and depositors' rights.

---

[2] Kabbara A.H. Ph.D Thesis op.cit., PP.296-300.

CHAPTER 12

Islamic Banking Theory

Islamic banking theory is mainly based on the abolition of interest and the introduction of profit and loss sharing (PLS) schemes and other methods of financing, such as iijara, murabaha, and salam sales. Currently Islamic banks consist of social, private, development, and international investment banks. The success of Islamic banking theory is manifested by its adherence to the Shari'a principles concerning financial transactions. First among these principles is the introduction of a new contractual relationship, a fiduciary relationship between the depositors as principals and the bank as manager trustee. Net profits are distributed among the depositors and shareholders while losses are shared according to each party's contribution. The relationship between the bank and the fund recipients is no longer a creditor-debtor relationship. The bank, as provider of funds, may become a partner in an enterprise financed through equity participation (musharaka) or trust fund (mudaraba). In this regard, we must distinguish between depositor-bank relationships (the liability side of banks) which is still largely mudaraba, and bank-businessman relationships (the asset side of banks), which is *mostly* murabaha and other sales-based financing. Thus the return on a bank's investment is not guaranteed nor do the depositors' funds yield a fixed return anymore. On the contrary, murabaha, ijara, and other sales-related instruments that generate a creditor-debtor relationship yield a margin or fixed return that is almost stable, if not guaranteed. Hence we observe that equity participation is *rarely* utilized as one would expect in an Islamic bank!

Objectives of the New System

Any task, especially of the magnitude to transform an interest-based economy into an Islamic one, must have a strategy, and any strategy should aim at a set of goals. However, neither the strategy nor the goals have any chance of being implemented without the aid of a set of methods and means to achieve the required objective (the abolition of interest) at the greatest possible benefits to society.

The abolition of interest is a major deviation from current and long-established economic policies worldwide. Changing the financial structure of the economy requires changing financial assets and obligations and these changes affect attitudes, concepts, and regulations.

The new approach for an alternative Islamic riba-free system is based on culture and beliefs that are deeply rooted in Islamic societies. Identification of the new system's objectives would contribute largely to a solid foundation for its implementation. These objectives are outlined as follows:

1. Emphasize the relations between Islamic norms and the direction and functions of the economy, including the banking system and the role of money.
2. Fill the gaps in the existing financial system and provide Islamic financing to all economic sectors, based on their needs, in accordance with a new development plan.
3. Establish a banking system based on profit and loss participation instead of the debtor-creditor relationship.
4. Create public awareness of the Islamic banking system and its benefits.
5. Create monetary policy and reorganize the control and supervision of the central bank in compliance with an interest-free economy.
6. Attract and promote long-term savings behavior in society.

As we have seen, Islamic financing methods such as murabaha and musharaka are used to finance foreign trade and working capital, while the needs of the business community for capital and durable goods can be met by ijara and leasing. Consumer financing can also be arranged through murabaha, ijara, or bai-salam.

Types of Financing Operations

In the conventional banking system, personal and corporate loans are performed through a simple financing mechanism. Banks, acting as financial intermediaries, accept deposits from the public and lend them to borrowers, regardless of whether these borrowers are individuals or corporate entities. The banks' profits are mainly attributed to the difference between interest expended (paid) to depositors and interest earned (received) from borrowers.

In the Islamic banking system the issue is more complicated. Money does not earn money without collaboration between capital and effort. Therefore depositors do not earn an automatic fixed return on their deposits as in the conventional system. A link has to be introduced so that the expected earnings of depositors are directly related to and constitute a proportion of the profits earned by the banks. Nonetheless, financing or participating instruments vary to suit the financial needs of the market and to provide short-, medium-, and long-term funds. These Islamic instruments take on one or more of the following forms: mudaraba, musharaka, murabaha, leasing, and *ijara wa'ktina*, istisna', salam, musaqa, and finally muzara'a. The definitions and mechanisms surrounding each of these are discussed below.

Mudaraba

Mudaraba (capital trust) is a pre-Islamic custom used to finance a significant portion of the caravan trade in the Arabian lands. Orientalists believe that commenda, as it came to be known in the West around the 10th century, was adopted from the Islamic commercial practice that was in operation as early as the sixth century. [1]

Mudaraba, in jurisprudence terms, is "a contract in profit sharing, with one party providing funds and the other his work."[2] In other words, mudaraba (or qirad) is a contract between two parties: an Islamic bank as an investor (*Rab al mal*) who provides a second party, the entrepreneur (*mudareb*), with financial resources to finance a particular project. Profits, if any, are shared between the two parties according to a percentage agreed upon in advance. Losses, if any, are the liability of the Islamic bank and the *mudareb* loses only his efforts.

The application of mudaraba in financing current Islamic banking operations is very limited owing to restrictions on mudaraba transactions and the tendency of bank management to avoid risk. These restrictions inhibit its wider application in covering many sectors of the economy. For instance, the majority of Islamic scholars argue that mudaraba should be limited to self-liquidating transactions.[3] Through such, the assets of the mudaraba are easily recognizable and must be realized and liquidated so that the proceeds can be easily distributed between the partners at the termination of operations, the completion of the deal, or the achievement of the mudaraba objectives.

If the partners want to renew the mudaraba, a new contract must be negotiated, but only after the old one has been terminated and the rights and liabilities of the parties concerned recognized and settled.[4] The Accounting and Auditing organization of Islamic Financial Institutions AAOIFI standards and most Shari'a scholars now fully approve constructive accounting methods for the liquidation of mudaraba. All Islamic banks use these methods in closing their year-end accounts and paying depositors their share of profits/losses.[2]

However, a broader definition of mudaraba, so that it may be applied to various economic activities, requires further research and thorough analysis. For one thing, the majority of Islamic jurists feel that mudaraba contracts should be confined to commercial activities. Nonetheless, this does not mean that new ideas and modern concepts must be shelved. On the contrary, the evolution and continuation of Islamic banking is largely dependent on innovative and new approaches to finance. New instruments or alternative financing modes can be created to conform to Islamic principles. Islamic banking and finance are new concepts in many respects and will not be harmed if new approaches are adopted, provided always that they serve the needs of modern societies and remain in compliance with Shari'a.

Musharaka Financing (Participation Financing)

Musharaka financing is a well-established partnership contract in Islamic law and was operational during the early Islamic era. It is also currently one of the more popular means of financing outside the banking system among commercial and small industrial sectors.

In the context of an Islamic bank, musharaka is described as a joint venture between an Islamic bank and a customer or business entity geared for certain operations. The venture may be terminated within a specified period of time or when certain conditions are met.

Unlike a mudaraba contract, the two partners in a musharaka participate in the capital of the venture

However, losses are borne by the partners in proportion to their capital contribution: For example, the bank may participate in 60% of the capital though its share of profits may not exceed 50%. In the case of losses, however, the bank's liability must not be less than 60%. The bank's right to ask for collateral or surety is limited by Shari'a for this type of financing.

The Islamic bank may finance industry, trade, real estate, contracting, and almost all legal enterprises through equity or direct participation. Musharaka is well suited for financing private or public companies and particularly for financing short-, medium-, and long-term projects. The Faisal Islamic Bank, Sudan, for example, finances selected projects and assists in the procurement of production equipment on a musharaka basis for periods up to three years. In all cases the projects are evaluated; if they are economically feasible and expected to be profitable and if the would-be partner has adequate experience and satisfactory references, the extent of the bank's participation can then be negotiated.

There are mainly two types of musharaka: (a) musharaka related to certain projects or deals and terminating with the project's completion and (b) redeemable musharaka. In the latter category, the bank recaptures the committed investment in proportion with the project's ability to generate profits and cash flow sufficient to pay back the bank's initial investment and the agreed percentage of profits. This type of deal is similar to redeemable participation in conventional banking systems.

Murabaha (Mark-Up on Sale)

Murabaha is an Islamic method for financing the purchase or import of capital goods, consumable goods, or raw materials. Under the murabaha agreement, the customer provides the bank with the specifications and quotations of the goods to be purchased. The Islamic banks study the documents with reference to the price, specifications, and conditions for payment. In many instances the bank would be able to obtain the same goods from a different supplier at more favorable terms than those obtained by the customer. When the bank and its customer agree on the terms of the deal, the former purchases the goods or commodities and then passes the title to the customer. The profit accrued to the bank is mutually agreed upon as a mark-up on the cost of purchase, with the following restrictions.

1. The purchase price should be declared to the client, especially when the bank succeeds in obtaining a discount or rebate. Since the mark-up is calculated on the net purchase price, any discount or rebate obtained has to be acknowledged and accounted for by client. This procedure is in strict adherence to murabaha rules.

2. Goods must be classified and clearly identified according to international or commonly accepted standards or classifications; otherwise murabaha contracts are void.

3. This element relates to whether the original agreement between an Islamic bank and the customer is binding or not. There are two methods to resolve this question. At Dar alMal alIslami an investment bank (DMI) the customer requests the bank to purchase the goods and submits intent to buy same on arrival. This promise is binding. At the Kuwait Finance House (KFH) the customer gives a non-binding promise to buy commodities that are purchased by the KFH on his behalf. Some scholars argue that the promise to buy the goods before the title is transferred and the goods are in the bank's custody cannot be binding for two reasons[1]:

   (a) I f the promise is binding, then the transaction would be similar to an ordinary letter of credit and the mark-up would be no more than disguised interest.
   (b) The occidental principle in Islamic contracts prohibits binding agreements whereby a party promises to deliver or sell goods he does not own.

However, the problem is resolved within Shari'a principles as follows:

   a) The promise or intent to buy will not be binding as long as the goods are not purchased.
   b) Custody of the goods is not always necessary since it is widely accepted that the bill of lading is the document of title in international trade. Once issued, an Islamic bank would be able to sign the sales agreement with the customer.

The transfer of title would be affected by endorsing the bill upon arrival of the goods at the port of destination.

Ijara (Lease Financing)

The exact meaning of the Arabic word *ijara* is reward or recompense. The use of ijara started before Islam and was regularized during the early zenith of Islam and has since been adapted to modern needs. A business or individual client may request that an Islamic bank purchase machinery or equipment with the intention of renting it to the client. Ijara financing is based upon valuing the client's financial position and the expected direct cash flow of the lease contract in the same manner as in ordinary lease financing decisions in a conventional bank, but without considering interest.

This instrument of financing has gained momentum in the conventional banking system owing in part to its tax advantages. In many countries rental payments are tax deductable.[5] Rental payments can also reduce zakat payments for liable companies, since if a leased asset is considered an article of trade, it is usually subject to zakat at 2.5%. An interesting question then emerges regarding whether leased articles of trade are exempt from zakat or not.

There are two forms of leasing in Islamic finance: (i) Direct leasing finance involves an Islamic bank allowing a customer to use its capital assets for a limited period ranging from a few days to years, depending on the type of assets in question. In return the customer pays a monthly or annual rental fee (i.e., an operating lease). (ii) In hire purchase (*ijara wa'iqtina'*) the Islamic bank rents assets to a customer who promises to purchase the assets within a specified period. The rental payment can be a certain fixed amount or a percentage directly related to the cash flow generated by the assets. The rental charges usually permit the lessor to amortize the assets and retain some profits (**financial lease**). The transfer of title depends on the nature of the deal. If a lump sum payment is agreed upon, the title will be transferred to the lessee upon exercising his option and paying the agreed price. If the payment is made in tranches and spread out over a period, the transfer of title will be gradual and the bank's title to the property, as well as the rental fees, will decrease proportionally with the successive payments of tranches.[6]

Istisna' Financing

The istisna' facility is a contract between a would-be buyer of products and the seller who will be asked to manufacture them. The buyer is called the *al-mustasne'h* and the seller is called the *al-sane'h*. The buyer could be the end user who arranges to finance the deal with an intermediary, such as an Islamic bank. Usually the financing contract stipulates the amount and terms of payment, either in one lump sum or by installments. A mark-up over the commissioned price will be the profits accrued to the bank.

This financing facility is not immune from risk, as reflected by the following potential problems:

1- Default in the payment of the principal amount and the mark-up when due.
2- Dissolution or liquidation of the *al-sane'h'* business before the goods are manufactured or delivered.
3- Misrepresentation by the *al-sane'h*.

The pricing of the Istisna' is supposed to compensate the bank for non-performance by the manufacturer. In addition, a penalty clause can be included to charge the *sane'h* for delaying delivery beyond the due date.[7]

A Suggested Formula for Istisna' Financing

According to this formula, the public authorities invite bidders to participate in the construction of a specified facility or a fixed investment project. The public authority will pay the price in installments. When the facilities are built and the *istisna' contract* is fulfilled. Ownership of the facilities is immediately transferred to the public authority against the deferred sale price. That price normally covers the construction cost and certain profit.

Salam Financing

Salam financing is a convenient and legitimate contract by which the Islamic bank advances payment, for example, to a farmer in compensation for agricultural goods to be delivered in the future (see Commodity Trading, below). This type of contract carries three types of risks, which may be the reason it is not a popular instrument.

First, the seller may default.

Second, the bank must liquidate the goods to redeem its money. This is done through selling the goods but, such a sale is not possible before effective possession.

Third, if the seller fails to deliver the goods on the due date, the bank cannot ask for compensation, unlike in istisna'.

Muzara'a (Share cropping)

Sharecropping is a partnership between a land owner and a farmer whereby the former provides land to the latter for cultivation and maintenance. The two parties divide the produced crop between them according to customary practices or mutual consent

Musaqa (Irrigation)

Musaqa is a partnership between a land owner and another party, usually a farmer. The land already contains trees and plants and produces edible fruits. The farmer undertakes to irrigate and maintain the crops in consideration for a share of the produce.

Commodity Trading

Generally commercial Islamic banks are currently involved in spot cash markets. Future contracts are permissible within the following boundaries:

1. Al-Salam (forward buying) requires full cash payments in consideration for goods to be delivered in the future. A salam contract stipulates the specific identification and determination of the commodities in terms of weight, measurement index, and duration of the contract.

The following types of sale are also allowed:

1. Tawliya (break-even sale), a sale at cost.
2. Wadia, a discount sale

Types of Financing by Maturity

Short-Term Financing

As we have seen, traditional methods of Islamic financing such as murabaha or musharaka are used to finance foreign trade and working capital. Mudaraba, musharaka, and Ieasing may be used for medium- to long-term purposes, while the needs of the business community for capital and durable goods can be met through ijara and leasing. Consumer financing can also be arranged through murabaha, ijara, or bai-salam.

Overdrafts and the discounting of bills and direct loans have no role in an Islamic banking system. While the discounting of bills has been practiced in Pakistan and Iran since the abolition of interest, according to the majority of *ulamah* (Shari'a jurists) this does not mean that they are lawful. An Islamic alternative for the discounting of bills by the central bank is discussed in Islamic monetary policy (see below).

Medium- and Long-Term Financing

Medium-term financing is defined throughout this chapter as financing with an initial term to maturity in excess of one year but not exceeding seven years, while longer-term financing involves terms to maturity in excess of seven years.

Equity financing, subordinated capital, and project financing are expected to be among the main instruments of medium- to long-term PLS schemes. Other instruments discussed earlier are trust finance (mudaraba) and participation finance (musharaka), istisna', and salam.

Equity Finance

Equity such as a stock is a claim against variable income. This definition applies to both the Islamic and conventional banking systems. At present commercial banks' lending portfolios consist of overdrafts, discounts, and straight loans. Though equity finance is not considered part of these activities, the banks hold equity ownership primarily in financial institutions and investment companies.

By contrast, if interest were to be abolished, equity finance would be one of the avenues for channeling funds to corporate borrowers. equity finance is but a form of musharaka between an Islamic bank and a corporation. Since this characteristic has not been tackled as comprehensively as it deserves in the Islamic literature, some explanation is needed. This development, taken alone (the transformation from lending to equity), makes radical changes in the banks' assets and liability structure and provides a new approach to financing. In this respect we have to differentiate between holding equity shares to maintain liquidity and holding them as a means of financing. Since equity finance inIslamic banks is meant to be a permanent share ownership as opposed to security trading, it should be matched with longer-term deposits.

In the absence of an Islamic capital market, direct equity finance would play a viable role in financing large and small firms in an Islamic economy. From the banks' point of view, equities are categorized by their development, investment, and venture capital means. Thus Islamic banks may provide financing through equity participation to serve various needs. For instance, to foster the development of an industry or any productive project, Islamic banks may purchase development shares issued by existing companies) to finance new expansion schemes or for modernization and rehabilitation. Banks can also finance venture capital by purchasing newly issued shares in high-tech companies or companies aiming to launch a new product or project.

Subordinated Capital

To the best of my knowledge, Islamic equity financing permits no subordination of one group over another in profit distribution or in liquidation. Subordinated capital, as the name implies, is a form of loan capital subordinated to other creditors, with an initial term to maturity and no restrictive covenants.[8]

Like many forms of Islamic finance, subordinated capital does not incorporate restrictive covenants. Thus the immediate difference between subordinated capital and equity lies in the distribution of returns, which is interest based under the conventional system and profit related under the Islamic system. However, subordinated capital is different from equity in that it has no voting rights and does not share in capital gains. Equally important, is that the bank is not liable for company losses in the conventional system, whereas it is under the PLS formula.[9]

Project Financing

Project financing is defined as a method of "financing an economic unit capable of generating sufficient cash flow to conservatively cover operating cost and debt services for a project over a reasonable time period which is less than the economic life of the asset."[10] Project financing has been especially important in capital-intensive industries such as those involved with oil exploration and development, mining, power plants, and transportation. It has helped in the last few years to provide unconventional and sometimes complex financing packages. Its complexities stem from the multiplicity of parties involved and the necessity to spell out and segregate the rights and responsibilities of each one. Venture capital is now a vibrant form of project financing that has great affinity with the spirit of Islamic financing.

Letters of Guarantee (LGs)

Principally, the issuance and acceptance of LGs are not a matter of dispute in Islamic banks. The controversy about LGs among Islamic jurists dwells on the situation when the fees charged on this service are proportional with the amount of the guarantee. The crux of the matter rests on the fact that according to traditional Islamic jurisprudence, the guarantee is a non-profit contract, which means that it must be given free of charge, as a "human service." According to traditional views, Islamic banks are prevented from taking proportional fees and are concurrently discouraged from rendering this service in order to avert risks that are not remunerated. Contemporary jurists classify the guarantees into commercial LGs and non-commercial LGs. Examples of commercial LGs are acceptance guarantees and performance bonds. Islamic banks are allowed to charge fees and commissions in compensation for the administration and paperwork involved in assessing the client's financial position, recording the transaction, and issuing the LG.

Meanwhile, banks are not allowed to charge the client in compensation for the risk involved. However, they may require the customer to cover about 2030 % of the guarantee and in return may issue the guarantee free of charge.

Transfer of Debts and Bill Collection

The transfer of debt was unknown in Roman law and it was not possible to transfer debt to a new debtor or creditor without liquidating the old debt and establishing a new debtor-creditor relationship, with new debt. Although it was possible to appoint a proxy to collect the debt, this was not an efficient disposition since the principal had the full power to cancel the proxy before the effective collection of debt.

Hawala, or the transfer of debt, dates back to the sixth century and became the basis for other financial instruments. While the transfer of credit was unknown in the European community until the enactment of the old

French Law, it was first introduced into the civil law in Germany in 1886 and in England partly in 1875 and finally in 1925.[11]

According to the *Larousse* French dictionary and the *Dalloz* French legal encyclopedia, the Arabic word *hawala* is the origin of the word *val*.

The collection of bills through Islamic banks is a legal act since collection is but a service rendered by the bank on behalf of the owner or endorser of the bill. The bank is entitled to obtain a fee or service charge for such work.

Bill Discounting

Discounting is the act of endorsing a bill of exchange by the beneficiary to a bank. In consideration thereof, the bank pays the beneficiary the amount of the bill, in advance, less the discount. Normally, the discount rate includes commissions and endorsement fees plus the interest rate on the value of the bill from the discount date to maturity. As explained earlier, there is no question regarding the validity of the service fee.

As for the interest charged by the bank, the International Fiqh Academy and many *Fuqaha* have ruled that bill discounting by a bank is not valid in Islamic jurisprudence for the following reason[12]

1. The transfer of debt from the endorser to the bank is not valid due to the inequality between the transferred debt and the debt to be collected.
2. By the same token, it is not a loan either, since the amount paid by the bank is less than that to be collected from the debtor.
3. It is also not a sale of debt due to the fact that the sales of pecuniary assets for same is only valid if an equal value of currency is exchanged for an equivalent value of the same or of another currency; otherwise the transaction would lead to riba al-fad'l.

Types of Notes and Means of Payment

There are three recognized types of notes or bills in Islamic financial dealings: the check, the bill of exchange, and the promissory note. A check is a note by which a drawer advises the drawer, normally a bank, to pay a specified sum of money to a third person, called the beneficiary. A bill of exchange is a commercial paper by which the drawer (the creditor) orders another person (the debtor) to pay a sum of money on a certain date to a designated beneficiary or to the bearer of the bill. A promissory note is an undertaking by the signatory to pay a specified sum of money, on a certain date, to a second person, called the beneficiary.

By the same token, trading and issuing certificates of deposit and bonds whether yielding fixed or floating rates of interest and whether convertible to shares or not is not allowed in Islamic banks. Zero-coupon bonds, which are bought at a discount, are also banned because the discount is merely the difference between the face value and the purchase price and represents the accumulated interest on the purchase price.

Social Services of Islamic Banks

Social services are considered an integral part of Islamic banking operations. In fact, in many Islamic banks, these an important function and not merely a by-product, as one might imagine.

These services may be classified into three main categories: benevolent loans (*qard hasan*) and overdrafts, the collection and distribution of zakat funds, *sadaqat* (donations), and, finally, the preservation of Islamic culture and heritage.

Summary and Recommendations

Trust finance (mudaraba), participation finance (musharaka), equity finance, and subordinated capital are non-debt modes of financing. They are a means of sharing ownership between a bank and client. The implementation of non-debt modes of financing should be subject to government regulations and supervision, since they are provided as a substitute for debt financing or even fixedyield instruments, known as sales-based Islamic debt-generating modes of financing. In addition, at all times the authorities should aim at maintaining freedom of contracting between banks and their clients in conformity with the Islamic law.

Direct alternatives to interest based conventional financing involve trade credit and equity financing modes. With trade credits, the seller finances the buyer by selling the buyer either goods or services on credit for a typically higher price than the cash price. The difference between cash price and the deferred sale is called a markup. In equity financing the financier provides capital and shares in the equity of a venture, to either gain or lose, depending on the outcome of the deal.

Finally, it is permissible to charge customers with direct fees for *banking services* that involve no extension of credit (are not debt based).

Endnotes:

1. A. L. Udovitch, 1970, pp. 171172.
2. A. Abu Gudda, "Mudaraba (qirad) and Modern Applications," in the Second Islamic Bank Conference, Kuwait Finance House, Kuwait, March 22-25, 1983, p. 6.
3. Sami H. Homoud, 1982, 2nd ed., 408-409. For an extensive coverage of mudaraba, see also pp. 388-417, and "Mudaraba" and "Mudaraba Company" in *Islamic Law Encyclopedia*, Vol. 10, pp. 388-417, Ministry of Awqaf and Islamic Affairs, Kuwait, n.d.
4. AAOIFI Sharia Standards No. 12 Sharika (Musharaka) and No. 13 Mudaraba, Bahrain, 2008. I am Indebted to A. Zarqa for pointing this out.
5. Sheikh Abdulhamid al-Sayeh, "Sales Contracts in Islamic Jurisprudence," Second Islamic Bank Conference, Kuwait, op. cit., p. 6.
6. Fiqh Academy Rule No. 7.
7. Future sales (b*aia al ajal*) require the transfer of goods to the buyer while payment due in the future and at a higher rate than in cash sales.
8. "The Measurement of Capital," Bank of England Bulletin, September, 1980. 1990 and 1992 Anas al Zarqa proposed a Shari'a compliant form of preference shares but until now the idea has not taken off.
9. United Nations Industrial Development Organization Workshop, Jamal Attia, "Islamic Financing Mechanism Available for Islamic Banks and the Need for New Mechanism," June 1986, p. 5.
10. Peter K. Nevitt, 1979, p. 167.
11. Attia, op. cit., p. 6.
12. Attia, 1986, pp. 5-6.

CHAPTER 13

Implementation of a Riba-Free Economy

Knowledge comprises (a) the concept (*tasawur*), which is apprehended by definition, and (b) the assertion or judgment (*tasdiq*), which is apprehended by proof.[1]

The strategy to transform an interest-based economy into an Islamic one should aim at a set of goals. Both strategy and the goals have no chance of being implemented without the aid of a set of methods and means to achieve the required objective namely the abolition of interest.

Since the abolition of interest is a major deviation from current and long-established economic policies worldwide it requires changing the financial assets and obligations. This affects attitudes, concepts, and regulations.

This chapter attempts to accomplish the following:

1. Define the economic goals of both the conventional and Islamic economic systems.
2. Compare the basic objectives of monetary policy in the conventional and Islamic systems.
3. Analyze the various instruments of monetary policy, with respect to Kuwait, including prudential regulations that could be construed as the abolition of interest.
4. Show the basic findings and conclusions that can be reached from such analyses.

Economic Goals

The fundamental function of the government is to stabilize the economy, which is mainly achieved through fiscal policy. The fundamental purpose of fiscal policy is to eliminate unemployment and inflation, which is achieved through its tools, namely, government spending, a public budget, and tax collection. Stability, however, does not mean stagnation, since the government, through adjusting public spending and taxes, aims to control inflation and stimulate economic growth.

Table 1.—Economic goals, by definition

Conventional[2]	Islamic
1. Economic growth An increase in real output.	Same, with the aim to develop more efficient and less costly techniques, introduced over time.
2. Full employment Suitable jobs should be available for all those willing and able to work.	Same
3. Economic efficiency Business executives, workers, and consumers should enjoy a high degree of freedom in their economic activities.	Efficiency is enhanced through the avoidance of *israf (lavish spending)*
4. Price stability Eliminate sizable upswings and downswing in general prices, that is, avoid inflation and deflation.	Same
5. Economic freedom	Individuals are free in their pursuit of economic activities without impinging on the interests of society (*jama'h*), as long as they produce or trade in what is permissible and abstain from what is forbidden (*muharram*).

6.	Equitable distribution of income No citizens should face bleak poverty while others enjoy *opulence.*	Same
7.	Economic security Provisions should be made for chronically ill, handicapped, aged, or otherwise dependent persons.	Same addition, provisions should be made to secure a minimum subsistence level for deprived citizens.
8.	Balance of trade A balance of trade should be achieved.	Same
9.	Improving the physical environment	Improving and maintaining the physical environment.

Monetary Policy Objectives

It appears that the main objectives of monetary policy in the Islamic and Western economies are almost identical. The main difference lies in the emphasis of policy. Islamic economists focus on internal stability in the value of money. Western economists are also concerned with stability and justice, with monetarists concerned with controlling the intermediate targets of the money supply and interest rates to curb inflation. In the monetarist's view, lower inflation reduces prices and increases demand, eventually leading to a reduction in the rate of unemployment.

A comparison between Islamic and Western monetary policies reveals that both systems have similar objectives, with minor differences (see Table 2).

Table 2. Monetary policy objectives

Islamic Economy[3]	Western Economy[4]
Stability in the value of money	Price stability
Economic well-being with full unemployment	Minimum employment

External stability...Satisfactory balance of payments

Optimum rate of economic.............................Maximum or stable growth growth

In terms of general economic policy objectives, both systems seem to stress the efficient allocation of resources and the equitable distribution of income. The priorities of an Islamic system are the elimination of poverty, the equitable distribution of income, and economic efficiency. While both systems agree on these principles, they differ in the ways and means to achieve their goals.

Prudential Regulations and Monetary Policy

Implementation of Islamic Monetary Instruments

The banning of interest and consequently the absence of a discount rate mechanism are basic features of an Islamic economic policy. These characteristics would not cripple monetary or prudential control. Besides, as explained later, the monetary authority would have to seek different monetary instruments from those applied in the conventional system. In the absence of empirical evidence, it is difficult to determine whether the importance and impact on monetary aggregates of such instruments would be as effective as conventional ones[5]. It is worth mentioning, however, that Islamic monetary theory and its instruments are not yet fully developed. This is to be expected, since the subject has only recently been tackled in the literature. In addition, it is too early to draw conclusions based on the functions of the Iranian and Pakistani Central Banks, since both are still in the experimental phase. However the Sudanese seem to have advanced in this field, thanks to International Monetary Fund (IMF) involvement and assistance.

Islamic monetary and prudential control would not be confined to liquidity and reserve ratios, for instance, we have Islamic open market operations, profit sharing rates ceilings on margins, capital adequacy ratios, self-imposed regulations, and selective control measures.[6]

In the absence of a discount window and conventional open market operations in an interest-free economy, monetary policy tools would not be limited. The authorities must seek powerful tools that are acceptable by Shari'a For example, controlling the money supply would be accomplished through central bank deposits, with member banks and floating PLS bonds the Islamic monetary authority could change the level of the money supply and thus exert the desired effect on the financing operations of member banks.

Monetary and Prudential Controls

It is essential at this point to distinguish between monetary control and prudential control or their regulations, as outlined below. It should be emphasized that the classification below is based on imposing a tool that differs from country to country. In addition, the liquidity and reserve ratios may be used for both monetary as well as prudential control or they may be used solely as a regulatory tool (e.g., the Bank of England is in favor of reintroducing the reserve ratio as a regulatory measure).

Monetary Control

Monetary control measures would normally include the following:

- Open market operations.
- Profit sharing ratios
- Ceilings on margins.
- Discount windows
- Reserve ratios.
- Liquidity ratios.

Prudential Control

Prudential control measures would normally include the following:

- Statutory regulations (minimum capital requirements, limitations on lending).
- Self-imposed regulations.
- Selective control measures.

The section discusses instrument variables with reference to Kuwait. Examples, where applicable, are taken from the Iranian, Pakistani, and Sudanese experiments in monetary policy and control, bearing in mind that there are significant differences in the economies of these countries. In addition, the banking sector is nationalized in both Pakistan and Iran, which is not the case in Kuwait or elsewhere in the Gulf region.

Open Market Operations

In the conventional system, government securities are a useful device for financing the government and replenishing the money supply and banks reserves through open market operations (selling and buying government securities to the private sector).

Since securities are generally an interest-bearing instrument (securities here refers to treasury bills, notes, and bonds) they cannot be used in deficit financing or open market operations in an Islamic system.

It should therefore be mentioned that treasury bills that are sold at a discount are no different from zero-coupon bonds or any other type of debt instrument. Evidently, the interest factor in treasury bills is the difference between the sale price and the nominal price at the time of issue. Afterward, the market price of the bill reflects the expected changes in interest rates, as well as the life of the bill (prior to the selling date).

Accordingly, it is to be expected that open market operations, as currently known, would be ruled out in conjunction with the abolition of interest, provided, of course, that an acceptable and widely available Islamic substitute is formulated.

The Sudanese Central Bank (SCB) enacted an Islamic finance sukuk lawin 1998. In its bid to manage monetary policy and liquidity in the economy, the SCB issued various types of sukuk to encourage open market operations such as:

1   Central bank musharaka certificates (Shamam)
    Shamam represents real assets owned by the SCB and the Ministry of Finance in profitable institutions. The certificates allow the owner to participate in the profit and loss of the underlying assets. The SCB employ Shamam in open market operations to manage liquidity. It is only transferable though between banks.[7]

2   Sudanese government musharaka certificates (Shahameh)
    This certificate differs from Shamam in two aspects:
    • It is transferable between public banks and other financial institutions.
    • It aims to finance budget deficits and may be traded in secondary markets.

3. Ijarah certificates (Shehab)
    *   The SCB securitizes its assets of ijarah and these are only transferable between member banks and not to the public. It is mainly used to manage liquidity in the economy.

4. Investment government sukuk (Sar'h)
    *   These sukuk are issued by the government and the SCB to finance medium- to long-term development projects.

Controlling Margins

This device refers to the margin that must be contributed by a borrower who seeks to finance a house purchase. The central bank may raise this margin in a bid to curtail demand or lower it to encourage buyers to apply for financing.

Profit Sharing Ratios

Mudaraba profits involve profit sharing ratios between an investor (*mudareb*) and a managing trustee. This rate is normally fixed by custom and the will of the parties. PSR is debatable among Islamic economists. Some Islamic scholars advocate that the Islamic central banks use this rate to manage liquidity in the economy. However, I do not believe it would be an efficient tool of monetary policy if it requires unwarranted intrusions on the will of the parties. In addition, the variety of such rates dictated by the type of musharaka and risks involved complicates the situation.

In addition advocates of using these ratios as a monetary tool do not specify a workable mechanism for such a policy, except to point out that it could be used to control the money supply and credit expansion.[8] Further research is needed to devise a framework for observation rather than manipulating the ratios by the bank.

Bill Discounting and the Discount Window

Commercial papers have traditionally been an accepted means of payment and are used in domestic and international trade (documentary bills). The use of documentary bills has grown in connection with imported goods and should be supported by other documents (e.g., bills of lading and insurance policy). When a bill is drawn, it may be discounted by a bank so that the seller (drawer) can obtain cash when needed rather than wait until the bill's due date. On the other hand, a bill can be drawn on a bank by prior arrangement with the buyer against acceptance credit (e.g., irrevocable documentary credit). Islamic scholars have concluded that drawing a bill is legitimate whereas discounting is not.

The bank discounting the bill profits from the difference between the amount it pays to the seller of the bill and the value to be received at maturity. The difference (discount) is calculated according to the market interest rate and time left to maturity. For example, a bill due in two months that has been discounted now, when the rate of interest is 12%, means that the seller of the bill has to pay 2% (2 x 12/12 x 100) in interest charges plus, of course, commission fees and other charges.

The central bank in Islamic countries and elsewhere rediscounts a significant portion of the commercial bills held by the banking system against a thin margin. Rediscounting improves the banks' cash position and allows them to increase credit expansion to various sectors of the economy. Perhaps the monetary authorities in Pakistan could not rule out bill discounting for these reasons.

The Central Bank in Iran (CBI) still buys and sells commercial papers and certificates of indebtedness. Such mechanisms could yield the same results as interest rates, insofar as the impact of monetary policy is concerned.[9] The mechanism of this policy has not been declared, however. Presumably commercial papers will be rediscounted by the central bank when the monetary authority aims to replenish the banks' liquidity. Nonetheless, this tool has no significant impact on the quantity of money in the economy.

The importance of discounting of bills to alleviate short-term liquidity problems in the economy unfortunately does not legitimize their sale at a discount in the view of Shari'a. A few contemporary scholars hold the view that bill discounting is accepted, since this transaction is similar to selling debts at a discount, which is permissible by the majority of scholars.

Selling debts at a discount is subject mainly to two conditions by Shari'a,

(i)   the sale of debt is permissible at its corresponding value and,
(ii) the sale price must be paid on spot

Any additional sum accruing from the sale is riba. This is in compliance with the Hadith narrated by Abd Allah Ibn Omar, who said: "I came to the Prophet and said, I sell a camel in al Baqi, with the price denominated in gold coins and collected in silver coins and all them in denominated silver coins and collecting in gold coins". The Messenger of God said," there is no harm if you take it at its spot price, as long as you do not depart without full concluding the transaction".[10]

Thus, bill discounting may not be legalized under these conditions. Its use as a monetary tool, however, stems from its acceptance as a negotiable instrument by banks and traders. Currently, commercial papers are readily discounted and rediscounted by banks in all Islamic countries, a process that is likely to be abolished if stringent application of Shari'a is adopted.

Monetary Policy in Kuwait

Monetary policy in Kuwait, as in Western economies, aims to achieve a broad range of general economic policy objectives, although the Kuwait economy is different in many respects from Western economies. First, there is no personal or corporate income tax, except for an initially 5% levy (then decreased to 1%) on the net profits of Kuwaiti shareholding companies, which is allocated to the Kuwait Foundation for the Advancement of Science. Second, there has been no need for government borrowing and since 1986 there has been no national debt.

Third, most of the government's revenue from oil investment income and treasury revenues is used to inject money back into the economy to finance current government expenditures and development projects. These characteristics of the economy eliminate some standard government tools of economic policy, such as tax incentives; alter others, such as money market operations via treasury bills; and make others more important, especially (a) the budget, which is concerned with the distribution rather than redistribution of the national product[11] and (b) the banking system and liquidity. However, central bank bills in Kuwait have little effect on credit expansion because they are part of the reserve ratio.

Fiscal Policy in Western Economies

Fiscal policy in the conventional system has changed from the days of *laissez faire, laissez vivre.* In modern times the state function of government in the economy has prompted economists to describe the current Western economic system as mixed capitalism. The recognized major goals of fiscal policy are as follows:

1- Redistributing income and wealth.
2- Adjusting the allocation of resources.
3- Controlling unemployment.
4- Controlling inflation.
5- Promoting economic growth.

The objectives of fiscal policy in Islam differ slightly in the means and tools used to implement such a policy as outlined, as shown below. Islam has are a leakage or withdrawal of potential purchasing power from the economy. In an Islamic state waste must be avoided as a spiritual duty and not merely as administrative prudence.

Fiscal versus Monetary Policy

There are four methods of financing in Western economies: (a) borrowing from the banking sector, (b) borrowing from the public, (c) taxation, and (d) progressive taxes (value-added tax).[12] Islamic economists, on the other hand, cite two ways an Islamic state can finance the government: (a) by issuing fiat money through the central bank against non-interest-bearing IOUs from the treasury[13] and (b) through taxation to finance normal expenditures (those that could not be financed by PLS arrangements).[14] By the end of 1986 neither of these two methods was applicable in Kuwait owing to the fact that the Ministry of Finance was a net creditor to the financial system and the main source of money supply in the economy.

The implementation of fiscal policy and the management of the state's reserves are currently under the Ministry of Finance. In the absence of meaningful income tax, income from oil is the main source of government spending. Since the early 1980s the government has chosen to finance persistent budget deficits by using up the general reserve.[15] If interest were abolished in Kuwait, the basic characteristics of its monetary policy objectives are expected to remain unchanged. These objectives include growth through the diversification of income (other than from oil), low inflation, the distribution of oil wealth, and the stability of the currency. As for the priorities of the new system, one can mention the endeavors to create a banking system capable of allocating resources to the benefit of those who need it most and to minimize the social cost of intermediation. The key to success of the new system lies in the positive implementation of these goals.

On the other hand, a few changes that were expected occurred in the main structure of the financial system precipitated by the abolition of interest, summarizedas follows:

a) The KFH and later on the newly established Islamic banks were brought under the supervision of the central bank. As of today, these banks are the Boubyan Bank, the Kuwait International Bank, the al-Ahli United Bank, and the recently come into existense government-sponsored Warba Bank.

b) It assumed that insurance companies would continue their operations as before the abolition of interest. As expected, solidarity companies established since the mid-nineties are working along with traditional insurance companies, performing their operations under Islamic principles.

Money and Capital Markets

This section focuses on describing the financial instruments available in the money and capital markets and their characteristics.

Money Markets

Generally, money markets provide borrowers with short-term capital and create an outlet for investors to employ their surplus funds. Moreover, developed money markets help channel domestic savings from investors to the ultimate users efficiently and with the lowest possible transaction costs.[16]

Money market transactions are restricted in the Islamic financial system. Call money, or overnight money, is not available unless it is obtained free of interest. The inaccessibility of short-term money to alleviate acute but not chronic liquidity shortages in the Islamic banks could be partially resolved through inter banking operations within the Islamic banking structure, as follows.

A cash surplus bank would furnish cash-deficit banks with fresh money in the form of sight or short-term deposits, with several deposits or withdrawals during the year. At the end of the year, the donor bank would share in the profits of the recipient bank along with the banks' savings or term deposit accounts. The method used in calculating the profits attributed to the donar bank is based on the daily point products. A second method of alleviating an acute liquidity shortages would be through the central bank's deposits, as mentioned earlier.

A short-term money instrument is therefore *not* lacking, though research on short-term money instrument is constantly being conducted to prove new accepted instruments at the Islamic Development Bank's (IDB) training institute. With technical help from the IMF, the Sudan has introduced two Shari'a compliant financial instruments suitable for monetary policy, Money market instruments of the conventional banking system, such as bankers' acceptances and LGs, are also issued in the Islamic system, gratis except for a service charge, regardless of the amount of the guarantee and against adequate surety.

As for Kuwaiti, a few Shari'a compliant overnight money is available whereas the market is dominated by the conventional type instruments. Additionally, the Kuwaiti Central Bank can provide emergency funds to Islamic banks for up to six months in conformity with Shari'a or sell and purchase short-term securities from Islamic banks. Kuwaiti conventional money market encompasses call and time deposits, four main categories of financial instruments: certificates of deposit, central bank bills, floating rate notes, and promissory notes. None of these instruments is interest free.

Capital Markets

In principle, an Islamic bank can underwrite securities and be active in trading and selling. Portfolio selection and equity participation are governed by rules and regulations that must be strictly followed: For example, (a) the company issuing the shares should not deal or trade in banned operations and should not be a financial institution whose main activities are directly related to trading in interest-bearing bonds, (b) dividends or yields must not be guaranteed or stated in advance, and (c) dealing in preference shares is forbidden on the grounds that they entitle the holder to preferential rights as to dividends and they bear a fixed rate of return.

Capital Market Instruments

The Kuwaiti capital market is characterized by a relatively unique feature in that the government is not a primary borrower in the market.

On the contrary, the government is a primary supplier of funds, not only indirectly through government expenditures and land purchases, but also through its direct purchases of public issues by banks and financial institutions in Kuwait and abroad. This characteristic may explain to some extent the government's initiative to establish a Kuwaiti banking market.

Prospects of the Capital Market

The evolution of an orderly Islamic financial market depends on the development of an Islamic financial structure in a given country or region. Fortunately, a number of opportunities for such development in Kuwait are currently available. First, there are surplus units looking for investment opportunities; conversely, there are deficit units looking for funds. Second, Islamic banks can issue financial claims, that is, deposits to the surplus units. These deposits become available to corporate or individual entities through intermediation. Third, the corporations issue shares that can be sold to the public or to Islamic financial institutions. The process of equity participation through shares is very popular in Kuwait. Fourth, there are virtually no restrictions on buying or selling company shares in the open market, except, of course, shares of closed shareholding or limited liability companies.

However, two important segments of the market are missing: trading in government securities and trading in corporate debt certificates. The development of these two instruments in the conventional system and of Sukuk in the non interest system is a cornerstone toward the evolution of the financial markets.

Islamic Sukuk

Islamic sukuk, or "investment sukuk," as labeled by the AAIOFI, are asset-backed securities issued in equal portions. The AAIOFI defines them as certificates utilized to finance certain projects (mainly infrastructure projects). Investment sukuk vary in type and can be either murabaha or musharaka certificates, including certificates of ownership of leased assets, certificates of ownership of usufructs in existing assets or services, istisna' or salam certificates, muzara'a, musaqa, or mugharasa certificates.[17]

The issuance of Islamic sukuk has developed very rapidly due to its safety cushion and reasonable returns, as well as due to the development of infrastructure projects that require Shari'a compliant long-term financing. This has prompted many Asian and European countries to issue legislation to organize and facilitate the issuance of sukuk and to even grant tax exemptions.

It is noteworthy that the Islamization of the banking system in Pakistan permitted the floatation of PLS certificates. This development was aided by the pre-existing financial infrastructure, including market makers and investment funds, and a set of rules and pertinent laws and regulations, such as the mudaraba ordinances.[18]

Characteristics of Investment Sukuk

Investment sukuk are issued in the name of the owner, or bearer, and as such represent a common share of the underlying assets, including services and usufructs. The returns of these investment sukuk are normally described in a prospectus, whereas losses are shared in proportion to the ownership share. There are two parties to an investment sukuk contract: the issuer and the subscriber. The issuer can be a firm, a financial institution, or the government. Trading these certificates is permissible through sales, pledges, gifts, and any other permissible transactions. On the other hand it is not permissible to securitize debts for trading purposes due to Shari'a objections in selling debts for debts.

The major types of sukuk issued in October 2012 were murabaha equaling $4.7 billion representing 53.3% of international sukuk followed by ijara amounting to $1.1 billion or 12.8%, musharaka $1 billion or 11.4% of total issued sukuk internationally, Government and semi-government issues constituted 61% of international issues and 20% for issues of the financial services sector and 5.5% in the construction sector.[19]

The Supervisory Authorities

Central Bank Supervision

Usually Islamic banks are established by special decree laws in their countries of incorporation, with the exception of the International Islamic Bank which was established in Denmark in 1983 under the Danish Banking

Act. In 1981, the governors of the central banks and representatives of the monetary authorities of the member states of the Islamic Conference agreed to put Islamic banks under the central banks' control.

To cope with the evolution of Islamic banks, the central bank in Kuwait enacted Section 10, which regulates the establishment of Islamic banks, and incorporated new modifications to Banking Law No. 32. Islamic bank, as defined by the Central Bank of Kuwait (CBK) is a joint stock company with assets of no less than KD 75 million that conducts financial and direct investment operations on its own account or in participation with other companies undertaking various economic activities (Article 86).

The law permitted Kuwaiti conventional banks to establish subsidiary companies to conduct Islamic banking. A subsidiary should have a minimum capital of KD 15 million, 61% of which must be kept by the founding bank (Article 87). The law also permits foreign Islamic banks to establish a branch in Kuwait with a minimum capital of KD 15 million (non-transferable). Each Islamic bank must have an independent Shari'a supervisory board to be elected by the general assembly. The Shari'a supervisory board is required to submit to the general assembly a report comprising its opinion of each bank's operations in compliance with Shari'a principles.

The CBK can assist in liquidity shortages by providing emergency funds to Islamic banks for up to six months through Shari'a approved instruments and methods. The CBK can also sell and purchase Islamic-oriented securities and other instruments from Islamic banks. In addition, the CBK can issue Islamic instruments when needed.

Central Banking and Monetary Policy

Among the central bank's main objectives during the transition period is to devise non-usurious banking law and regulations. The central bank's main function would be modified to cope with the requirements of the new system. For example, its refinancing or recurrent deposits with member banks would be on a PLS basis. The profit ratio awarded to the central bank would be lower than that accorded saving accounts for banks' profits rates on specified mudaraba contracts.

The abolition of interest is not expected to change the objectives of Kuwait's monetary policy, which include growth through the diversification of income (other than from oil), the efficient allocation of resources and distribution of wealth, low inflation, and the stability of the currency.

Religious Supervisory Board (RSB)

To ensure conformity with Shari'a requirements, an Islamic bank usually has an RSB that supervises and controls its activities in various ways, such as the following:

1. The RSB reviews each type of contractual arrangement with a depositor and each type of investment to be undertaken by the bank.
2. The RSB assists in the interpretation of Shari'a to ensure that the bank's investments are Shari'a compliant.
3. The RSB must approves all financing schemes and various contracts, agreements, policies, products, financial statements, and reports among Islamic institutions and their prospective partners, clients, or other entities.
4. The RSB "performs" a Shari'a audit and "issues" an annual audit report of its findings to the central bank and shareholders.

The AAOIFI

The AAOIFI was established by Islamic financial institutions on 1 Safar 1410/1990 as an autonomous non-profit organization. Its objectives are to

- Develop accounting and auditing opinions.
- Incorporate accounting and auditing standards in accordance to Shari'a principles.
- Conduct seminars, conferences, and training courses to clarify and justify newly released accounting and auditing standards.

Higher Committee for Shari'a Supervision

In 1992 the Sudanese central bank created the HCSS, an independent body working in collaboration with the central bank. Its main tasks are to

- Supervise and follow up Shari'a principles among Islamic banks and financial institutions, including the central bank.
- Issue fatwa and resolutions to implement Shari's principles.

Islamic Financial Services Board

The IFSB is another independent international counsel, established in Kuala Lumpur in 2003. It is entrusted with issuing, supervising, and maintaining auditing standards in accordance with Shari'a principles. It also strives to maintain stability in the Islamic financial services industry. To support its objectives, it holds conferences, seminars, and training sessions.

Recent Developments

Last November 2010 the CBK met with the treasury managers of Kuwait's Islamic and conventional banks to discuss interbank transactions. The CBK urged the banks to step up interbank transactions, especially murabaha, between conventional and Islamic banks. Two conventional banks were hesitant on the grounds of the high risk due to the price escalation between buying the commodity and reselling it. However, the CBK was not convinced and urged the two banks to step up their murabaha transactions, since all the other banks were active. Furthermore, CBK explained that the risk involved was minimal due to the speed at which the transaction takes place. In addition, the CBK suggested the unification of murabaha contracts among member banks, subject to Shari'a rulings, which would ultimately decrease the level of risk, but mainly among conventional banks. Unfortunately, the Islamic banks declined this proposal on the grounds that each bank has a separate Shari'a board, such that each bank would have independent Shari rulings, which might differ slightly from one board to another.[20]

Therefore the supply of money as a target variable may be difficult to control (unlike the case in advanced economies) due to the interaction and sometimes contradiction between fiscal and monetary policies. Accordingly, economic activities cannot be controlled by monetary policies alone. Both fiscal and monetary policies must work in tandem to achieve long-term stabilization and progress. This also applies to the period immediately following the abolition of interest, insofar as the conditions prescribed above remain unchanged.

Summary

Economic development, the diversification of income, and the efficient allocation of resources and distribution of wealth are Kuwait's broad economic policy objectives. Monetary and fiscal policies are means to an end, namely, to achieve the stated objectives. The monetary authorities have been unable to effectively control Kuwait's base money because (i) the Ministry of Finance determines the government deposits with the central bank and (ii) the central bank's net foreign assets depend on its balance of payments.[21]

Endnotes:

1. As stated by M. Al-Ghazali in Montgomery Watts, *The Faith and Practice of M. Al-Ghazali*, George Allen & Unwin, London, 1953, p. 35.
2. Cambell. McConnell and Stanley L. Brue, *Economics*, 11th ed., McGraw-Hill, Baskerville 1990 p. 7.
3. For more details see M. Arrif, ed., *Monetary and Fiscal Economics of Islam*, 1982.
4. For more details see Douglas Fisher, *Money Banking and Monetary Policy*, p.243.
5. Bashir (1984) has studied the minimal ratios desirable for the Faisal Islamic Bank of Sudan so that it does not decrease the availability of loanable funds or affect the objective of optimizing the return to deposits and shareholders.
6. Kabbara, "Islamic Banking: A Case study of Kuwait" unpublished doctoral dissertation, Loughborough university of technology, Loughborough, 1988, p. 338.
7. Saber M. al Hassan, "Role of Supervisory Authority in Shari'a Control, Sukuk and Other Tools," Al Baraka Group.
8. Siddiki, 1986, p. 31, and Uzair in Ariff, p. 252. already cited.
9. For the impact of the new banking system on the instrument of "Monetary and Credit Policy in Iran." CBI International Seminar, op. cit., p. 13.
10. Al Sad'r, 1981, pp. 153-161.
11. Khouja and Sadler, op. cit.
12. Alvin H. Hansed, *Monetary Theory and Fiscal Policy*, McGraw Hill, New York, 1949, p. 167.
13. For example, see al-Jarhi in Z. Ahmed, 1983, p. 69.
14. Chapra, op, cit., p. 192. He also proposes to divert up to 25% of the banks' demand deposits to the central bank to finance socially oriented projects.
15. Khouja and Sadler, 1979, p. 162.
16. For more details see Jack Revel, *The British Financial System*, Macmillan Press, London, 1973, pp. 20-71.
17. For more details see AAIOFI, Standard No. 17, May 2003.
18. D. M. Quereshi, "The Role of Shari'a Based Financial Instrument in a Muslim Country," Kuala Lumpur Seminar, 1986.

19. Al Rai daily, Kuwait 7 Nov 2012, p. 48
20. *Al-Rai Daily, "Interbank Transactions", no author,* Sunday, November 7, 2010, Kuwait.
21. Khouja and Sadler, op. cit., p. 119.

PART III

THE IMPACT OF A
RIBA-FREE ECONOMY

CHAPTER 14

The Efficiency of a Riba-Free Economy

Efficiency is used here in a broad rather than a narrow economic sense. In a broad sense an efficient financial system is that which is capable of achieving the objectives of intermediation. These objectives range from facilitating the payment mechanism, providing a wider range of financial and advisory services, and in meeting the needs of both savers and investors. Potential efficiency in the narrow economic sense focuses on certain issues in the Islamic system and compares its efficiency with the conventional system. For example, a variable rate of return is compared with fixed rate of return to establish which of these rates leads to more savings than the other.

Microeconomic Efficiency of the Islamic Financial System

Range of Financial Instruments

The preceding chapter describes the financial instruments that exist and that could be introduced to Kuwait and elsewhere to provide a wider range of Islamic financial services. It also concludes that Islamic finance is able to meet the needs of deficit units and fund recipients (consumers and firms) for short-, medium-, and long-term financing, provided, of course, that all accepted financial instruments are fully operational.

Savers also have a broad range of investment outlets, such as savings and term deposit accounts, share and equity participation, and a limited number of Islamic investment certificates (e.g., PTCs, islamic sukuk covering musharaka, murabaha, salam, istisna', muzara'a, wakalah, leasing, and hire purchases). Instruments to choose from may include traderelated investments in the form of specified deposits and low-risk Islamic certificates (e.g., murabaha, qirad, and real estate). An Islamic qirad bond is an income-backed security through the revenue of a specified product. Commercial enterprises and consumers alike can acquire goods on murabaha. Other types of products, such as leases, istisna', and salam for financing inventory on credit sales, are also available (see Chapter 12). There are still other products, such as mudaraba contracts, whereby capital is contributed by one party while management is entrusted by an entrepreneur. There are also musharaka contracts where two or more partners share ownership and management.

As in interest-based systems, there is a wide range of financial instruments and new innovations thereof. However, many Islamic instruments are not yet fully developed or tested and must still be subjected to Shari'a constraints. This would constitute a considerable barrier for the Islamic financial system if interest were to be abolished before the final resolution of many technical and legal questions surrounding certain instruments, or at least before the provision of substitutes. It should be noted, however, that Shari'a constraints are not arbitrary and are intended to serve higher social and economic goals.

The Risk of Traditional Forms of Islamic Finance

The financing of businesses in the industrial, commercial, and other sectors of the economy by murabaha or musharaka methods carry some risk, for it ties up Islamic banks' returns on investment with the results of the operations of these businesses. In the case of dwindling returns, Islamic banks' profits may be affected proportionally to the ratio of their equity participation or PLS schemes in the overall financing operations. In addition, the degree of risk is normally associated with the type of financing instrument employed.

Islamic banks assume more risk in mudaraba finance than in musharaka, provided everything else remains the same. The high degree of risk associated with the former type of finance stems from the fact that Islamic banks provide 100% of the mudaraba capital and are entirely liable for any losses. Of course, in cases of fraud, mismanagement, or negligence, the managing partner would be fully accountable for his conduct and the bank would be entitled to fair compensation. Another risk consideration is the inadmissibility of collateral in mudaraba contracts.

Islamic jurists contend that the mudaraba contract and the capital entrusted to the *mudareb* is "trust money" and thus any request for collateral or guarantee against commercial risk renders the contract void because the contract is supposed to be based on trust between the two parties. However, the Hanbali school (a branch of the Hanafis), ruled that the stipulation of guarantee only constitutes a breach of the terms of the contract, which could be rectified without the need to nullify the contract itself, which remains valid. Nevertheless, it is permissible to request collateral to compensate the bank for damages resulting solely from the managing partner's negligence or misconduct. This implies that, in the absence of fraud or negligence, any losses are the outcome of adverse business conditions. Such uncontrollable circumstances have nothing to do with either the managing partner or the bank. It would therefore be unjust if the entrepreneur were to lose his time and effort and at the same time protect the bank against business losses.

Risk and Mobilization of Savings

One of the main parameters for judging a financial system's efficiency is its ability to mobilize savings. Islamic banks have generally been very successful in this regard. For example, the first Islamic bank experiment, in Mitt Ghamr, demonstrated how Islamic banking can attract deposits from the rural population and the role of banks in society and in 1983 the KFH stopped taking deposits because their inflow was more than the bank's processing capacity. What follows is a discussion of the effect of risk on the mobilization of savings and how It has been alleged that the first major weakness of Islamic finance relates to the high risk exposure for savers. Normal risk varies with the type and duration of assets. Demand deposits are the safest and almost risk-free. Savers only can access their deposits on demand, but the deposits are secured by the banks in compliance with Islamic law. This does not mean, however, that demand deposits would be automatically protected after the abolition of interest without enacting the necessary laws.

While demand deposits are risk free, they nonetheless have an opportunity cost representing lost returns that might have otherwise been earned from investments. Moreover, it would not be acceptable if most savers were to maintain idle balances to escape risk, since this would constitute hoarding (see Chapter 9, The Demand for Money in an Islamic Economy). A rational saver will not hold cash balances other than for transactional demands and emergencies; otherwise his balance would be eroded by zakat and inflation (resulting in a decline in purchasing power).

The subject of the indexation of benevolent loans is still debated in Islamic circles. However, the International Fiqh Academy generally rejects indexation and has issued resolutions on the matter. Various obstacles arise from the difficulty in selecting a workable index and the unavailability of up-to-date statistical data. Additionally, if a loan is to be adjusted upward to compensate for the rate of inflation, would this mean it should also be adjusted downward in the case of deflation?[1] Investment deposits are not likely to be fully guaranteed, since the current consensus in the Islamic literature is that investment deposits are similar to mudaraba capital and therefore the recovery of deposits must not be guaranteed by the banks (see Chapter 2). It is clear that in mudaraba, the scale of risk to savers includes the possibility of losing income as well as a portion of the deposited capital.

An investment in shares also offers reasonable returns commensurate with risks. It has been proven mathematically and empirically that the diversification of investments tends to minimizes risk. For instance, the variance of average stock returns decline as the portfolio grows until the variance becomes zero.[2]

The Impact of Risk on the Supply of Funds

This section analyzes the relation between the volume of financing and risk, as well as the risk of equity financing in an Islamic country such as Kuwait.

Another aspect of financial system efficiency is its ability to provide capital, irrespective of the volume of finance required and without bias against risk, as long as the investment is potentially profitable.[3] Islamic banks are well prepared to finance risky projects since they are under no obligation to pay a fixed return to their depositors.

Financing risky projects requires careful evaluation of the venture and the risk involved. A proper appraisal of the risks involved in an enterprise would take into consideration several factors, including profitability, management, ownership, and markets. Choosing profitable projects leads to securing the highest return to society. or the most socially desirable projects, government subsidies and policy incentives would ensure that sufficient resources are channeled to productive projects that need financing most.

Financiers sometimes want to finance a project that is capable of surviving on its own. This sounds reasonable in the case of individual companies, but when an enterprise is part of a larger group, it does not really matter much if a reasonable amount of risk is expected. Bain even says that: "an efficient financial system would therefore be characterized by the absence of any bias against risky investment projects."[4] The dangers of equity finance, however, can be very real in times of recession, depression, or sluggish demand for a company's products (or any other reason). In such instances, the banks' return on investment would decline and hence so would the depositors. There is nothing much the banks can do about it, nor the companies, other than to hope for better results in the future. When distributing dividends, some companies try, as a rule, to reduce sharp yearly fluctuations. The same policy could not be adopted if banks were to share in profits at a fixed rate.

Banks can, however, minimize the potential risk of loss in equity finance by limiting their equity participation (or even PLS financing in general) in the same company or the same group of companies. Moreover, banks can reduce the risk of PLS financing by using murabaha and ijara contracts, which bring an element of stability to their earnings and reduces the risk to their depositors. However, if investors are risk averse the PLS system distributes risk more equitably than an interest-based system.[5]

Equity capital is growing more popular as a conventional financing method. For instance, Pringle has pointed out that equity capital has accounted for the rapid growth of several of the newer merchant banks and is narrowing the differences between merchant banking and the work of industrial or commercial holding companies.[6] In addition, Auerbach has indicated that what matters is the expected return on investment, rather than the risk attached to it.[7]

Competition and Choice

The "extent" of free competition is another indication of the efficiency of a financial system. A free market economy relies heavily on competition to secure allotment efficiency, which occurs when the investment yield to society is likely to be at its highest level.[8] To what extent does this apply to Kuwait[9]?

First, competition among commercial banks in Kuwait is expected to be as keen after the abolition of interest as it is at present. Second, savers would have almost the same financial outlets as presently, such as banks, specialized institutions, investment companies, and the stock market. Although Kuwaiti insurance companies do not offer investment vehicles like their British or American counterparts, their investment operations would have to be modified to comply with the abolition of interest. Their insurance activity, however, may still be run as usual but is expected to decline in the face of a growing comprehensive Islamic insurance system.

Savers can currently switch from commercial banks to Islamic banks or to specialized banks, with the exception of the spelled out risk, since it is not a deposit taker, although it can sell certificates of deposit to the public. Consumer choice would not be limited in the Islamic financial system. Social loans could still be obtained from savings and credit banks, as is the case currently. Moreover, it is envisaged that commercial banks will improve their social loans as well, motivated by a greater awareness of their social responsibility to the community.

Banks would be able to gear interest-free deposits directly for benevolent loans. It is further expected that the banks with the highest number of social loans would gain a competitive edge in the market in terms of deposits. The above sources would also provide consumer financing.

Small and medium-sized companies are likely to encounter difficulties financing their operations if the current attitude prevails after the abolition of interest. In the past, small-scale industries had limited access to cheap industrial loans from the Industrial Bank of Kuwait, despite management's attempts to create a workable formula and establish flexible lending criteria. Part of the problem was in identifying small industries and the administrative resources needed to evaluate potential projects. These obstacles have only partially been overcome since the formation of a specialized company, the Industrial Investment Company for financing small- to medium-sized projects which was replaced by the formation of an SME fund by the government in 2013 with an authorized capital of KD 2 bn. More effort is still required in catering to small and medium-size businesses.

If the current practices and circumstances do not change, small commercial firms would face difficulty after the abolition of interest in obtaining seed capital from commercial banks. This is due particularly because of (a) the absence of a proven track record of sales and profits due to the lack of proper accounting data, (b) conservative traditional banking practices precluding the use of mudaraba or musharaka financing, (c) the lack of availability of collateral or sureties (the need for collateral would be significantly reduced, since it would be requested in trade-related finance but not in musharaka or mudaraba), and, (d) the fact that banks have to rely heavily on the honesty and character of the entrepreneur.

Thus, it seems that small firms would be at a disadvantage. The solution lies in changing the attitudes of the banks, coupled with direct government measures. One possibility is the government's establishment of a special fund for small businesses. The purpose of this fund would be to finance small firms by providing, for example, 50% of the financing, with the rest financed by banks and private capital. This policy, if adopted, would widen the distribution of resources. Many small firms and sole proprietorships would then have access to external finance, which was previously inaccessible on religious grounds. This proposal was presented by the author several years ago. Luckily the government of Kuwait has established in 2012 an SME fund with KD 2 billion capital.

The Macroeconomic Efficiency of the Islamic Financial System

The criteria for examining macroeconomic efficiency involves an investigation of the effect of Islamic financing on aggregate savings and investments, as well as macroeconomic stability, followed by i) the effect on savers and investors' behavior and ii) the impact of zakat on savings, consumption and income.

Aggregate Savings and Investments

The current nature of the economy and government attitudes may greatly influence the prospects of interest-free banking. It is assumed, therefore, that an Islamic government will pursue a positive role in the financial sphere and may even be keen to create a desirable atmosphere for the new system. This assumption is very important for our analysis because if we study the effect of PLS on the level of savings, we are concerned with aggregate savings rather than individual savings.

It has not been proven that the elimination of risk-free assets would decrease aggregate savings. In other words, the existence of a rate of interest does not change aggregate savings in the economy. Individual savings, on the other hand, are more affected by the level of income rather than by interest rates. It is true, however, that, given a choice, individuals would prefer a fixed rate of return rather than a variable one, provided that the mean rate of return is the same. Additionally, given a certain degree of risk aversion and assuming that the rates of return after investing in risky assets are the same as before the introduction of risk, then obviously savings will decline. This is the result of a theoretical study by Nadeem Ul-Haque and Abbas Mirakhor[10] These authors' most crucial finding is that by the elimination of all risk-free assets and the introduction of risk assets, wealth owners would try to restructure their portfolios to decrease the risk level rather than decreasing savings or investments[11]. This could be accomplished by holding low-risk assets as opposed to risk-free assets.

Studying the impact of uncertainty on savings, we examine the behavior of savers concerning the effect of uncertainty on both income and wealth as perceived by some prominent economists. Irving Fisher (1930)[12] and Boulding[13] assert that uncertainty about future income increases the propensity to save.

In their view, the risk of future income induces people to increase savings out of current consumption to guarantee for themselves the same level of income (or returns). Sandmo (1970) distinguishes between capital and non-capital income and argues that savings behavior varies with respect to the case under study. He finds that the overall impact of increased capital risk is likely to be indeterminate, since the substitution effect reduces savings when its yield is uncertain, whereas the income effect tends to increase savings.[14]

Waqar[15] (1985) shows the superiority of the variable rate system over the fixed rate system and that aggregate investments may be higher given a certain set of assumptions, namely, the following:

- Moral hazard is absent, the Islamic scheme does not have any collateral requirements, and investors are risk averse.
- Both financiers and entrepreneurs share the same views about the probability distribution of returns on investment.

More relevant to this analysis is Friedman's permanent income theory. The permanent income hypothesis suggests that people do not adjust their spending habits in conformity with their fluctuating or seasonal incomes. They treat their income as a smooth flow over a given period. According to Friedman, consumer spending and savings patterns are directly affected by consumers' permanent income rather than by actual though fluctuating money income. People weigh their savings, investments, and spending decisions according to their expected future income. Thus, they smooth their current spending/savings behavior, saving in prosperous years and "dipping into their savings in others."[16]

Nadeem Ul-Haque and Abbas Mirakhor[17] in 1987 expected a *shift* from a capitalist to an Islamic interest-free economy (IIFE) and concluded the following:

(a) The elimination of risk-free assets (interest-based loans) tends to increase the uncertainty of returns on savings in the face of variations in riskiness *and* the rate of return. Savings tend to decline "if the rate of return when risk is present is no more than the rate of return when risk is absent" (p. 137). Unless an Islamic economy generates better returns, eliminating interest, being equal, reduces savings.

(b) The reinforcement of Islamic precepts on the utility function and behavioral norms affects consumer decisions. Anas Zarqa summarizes the teachings likely to increase savings, such as the Islamic emphasis on i) moderation in consumption, (ii) inheritance that provides financial help, (III) self-reliance so as not to require financial help.[18]

Nonetheless, some economists are concerned that the elimination of interest would so adversely affect aggregate savings as to decrease investments, hinder efforts to reduce poverty, and discourage growth. Some even think that zero interest may lead to zero savings.[19]

After the abolition of interest, investments in productive activities and their financing will be managed without interest on loans. The past does not support the pessimist apprehensions, nor does the present, given the resilience and strong, innovative spirit demonstrated by the Islamic finance industry. In view of the above, it would be unrealistic to assume that a wholly equity-based system would lead in the future to instability in the banking sphere and the entire economy.

The Effect on Savers' and Investors' Behavior

Much of the criticisms regarding the effect of an interest free system on savings argue that aggregate savings would decline. Pryor, for example, argues the following[20]:

(a) Investing "passively" in an interest-yielding bond is not possible in a PLS economy and direct investment increases risk, leading to a drop in savings.
(b) Assuming that income and substitution effects (between current and future consumption) are the same in Muslim countries as they are in the West, savers would choose current rather than future consumption, thus contributing to a decline in current savings.
(c) The institution of zakat and the emphasis on charitable spending reduce the incentive for savings, particularly since zakat must be paid whether income is earned or not.

It is true that Islamic bonds are, to date, not widely available. However, it is possible, for example, to buy real estate bonds that yield stable income from many Islamic banks. Low-risk murabaha bonds are available from the IDB, although only in large denominations.

The Third World debt crisis and the "Kuwait" stock market crash have shown that direct investments are safer than many other types, which has prompted Citibank's chairman to declare that direct investments in Brazil are better than lending to the central bank.[21]

Ul-Haque and Mirakhor[22] show that in the Islamic system, given the assumption that the rate of return on PLS increases with the increase in risk, total savings will not be changed and may even increase. Then savings may decline, given the same level of risk in both the conventional and Islamic systems, if the rate of return drops after the abolition of interest. Waqar's[23] mathematical analysis is discussed below (see the section Efficiency) and it suffices to recall that he shows that under certain assumptions aggregate savings would increase in an Islamic system.

The spirit of the Islamic view of investment can be gleaned from two sayings of the Prophet

> "Even if the world is coming to an end, and you have in hand a sprout (scion), plant it if you can!" (Related by Al-Albani, No. 371) "A Muslim who plants a tree will earn a reward (from God) for anything eaten from it by a human, an animal or a bird, till the Day of Judgment." (Related by Muslim in his al Sahih No. 552)

The Impact of Zakat on Savings, Consumption, and Income

Regarding the point Pryor raised about zakat, the effect of zakat on savings is positive, given the fact that it induces investments such that it will not wipe out idle wealth (see the section on Demand for Money). Kahf has also found that zakat increases the rate of saving. The author points out that if an individual wants to keep his wealth constant after a payment of zakat, the "wealth-owner consumer" must increase his savings at a higher rate than the zakat rate to prevent his wealth from decreasing.[24]

Pryor (1985) simplifies Kahf equations by showing that if the rate of zakat on wealth, w, at the beginning of the same period, plus any net savings at the end of the period, we have the equation $w_{t+1} = (1 - z)(w_t + s_1)$. Deriving it with respect to s, one can easily demonstrate that the zakat levy increases savings at a much higher rate than the zakat rate of 2.5 %.[25]

Undeniably, the effect of zakat on recipients is positive, since it raises their disposable income. Depending on the recipient's income level, zakat leads to an increase in spending, but savings could also be expected to increase. Even if we assume that the recipients of zakat in the lower and higher income strata would increase their spending on basics and conventional necessities, respectively, aggregate savings would increase.

One may wonder whether Islam encourages economic enterprise and investment. Another would argue that Savings may not translate into investment but remain dormant in hoards. This preposition is actually discouraged morally, and more importantly institutionally, as the imposition of Zakah on liquid assets prods them to become investable funds. This tends to increase the supply of investable funds out of any given level of aggregate savings. Wealth owners must increase their savings/investments at a higher rate than the zakat rate, as mentioned above. This has been explicitly recognized since the earliest days of Islam. "Trade in orphans' funds, lest zakat eats them up," admonished Umer the second Caliph and several companions of the Prophet. Several schools of fiqh take this not only as wise advice but also as expressive of Shari'a rule.[26]

Islamic teachings clearly encourage productive activities, and investment both commercial and philanthropic (as in Waqf).[27]

Metwally demonstrates that under certain zakat conditions, a Muslim saver can undertake real investments, even when the expected rate of return is *slightly* negative. One cannot simply say that zakat is paid whether income is earned or not! For example, investments in fixed assets and negative income are exempt from zakat according to some jurists.[28]

The effect of zakat on aggregate savings and consumption has been criticized for the notion that zakat raises aggregate consumption, leading to a decline in aggregate saving. These views can be summarized as follows[29]:

1. Current economic research has not yet reached a definite opinion concerning the impact of the redistribution of income on aggregate consumption and savings.

2. The average propensity to consume among lower-income earners is not always greater than among higher-income earners.

3. Zakat is sometimes used to finance the purchase of capital equipment rather than for consumption, leading to more investments. Even if we assume that these investments will ultimately increase consumption, the ratio of investment to consumption is unknown.

4. There are three categories of recipients (the zakat administrators, those whose support of Muslims is needed, and warriors for God)

and they are not necessarily poorer than zakat payers. Thus their average propensity to consume is not necessarily higher than that of zakat payers.

5. Zakat increases the incentive to invest. This leads to an increase in total income to employment levels, which raises the consumption of low-income earners

However, it cannot be said with certainty whether the new consumption-to-income ratio would be higher or lower than the old one, that is, before the zakat levy.

Hence, the effect of zakat on aggregate consumption and aggregate income cannot be denied (due to the effect of zakat on investment leading to an improvement in the income and productivity of the poor). Additionally, it is difficult to predict whether the ratios of aggregate consumption and aggregate savings to aggregate income would increase or decrease after the imposition of zakat.[30]

Notably, Shari'a constraints are not arbitrary and intend to serve higher social and economic goals.

Macroeconomic Stability

Considering that our Islamic finance model is not totally equity based and the microeconomic efficiency factors outlined in the preceding section, it appears that the effect of an interest-free economy on stability should be readdressed to reflect the impact of the new financial system on macroeconomic stability. The criteria used to assess this include market stability, stability in fund prices, structural stability, and the new system's contribution to economic activity. Rather than to confine the analysis to earnings stability alone or to depict the flaws of an interest-based system to conclude that the interest-free system is better.

Stability of Earnings

Interest rates fluctuate and follow a cyclical pattern, increasing during business expansions and decreasing during recessions. The exact timing of each fluctuation is unpredictable, however. Thus volatility of interest and difficulty in predicting interest rate behavior lead to instability in the price of capital, or yield. If kept within a narrow range, interest volatility does not necessarily lead to instability in the whole system, although it increases uncertainty and complicates investment decisions.

Similarly, the rate of return in an equity based system exhibits a cyclical pattern, increasing during booms and declining in depressions. The changes in the level of return do not have an undesirable impact on structural stability if the changes are moving upward. Structural stability here means the financial system's ability to protect itself against failure. Only when profits decline or losses occur on a nationwide basis would stability be affected. Uncertainty in profits is very much a function of business risk and the state of the economy rather than the type of financing employed.

Therefore, financing in PLS does not change the level of uncertainty and the questions to be answered in equity finance are who takes the risks and how they are distributed. Thus, a PLS system allocates, more equitably, the uncertainty among all depositors in a bank. This leads to greater stability since each party, according to Zarqa, "can absorb its modest share of a loss without significantly upsetting its normal activities or defaulting on its obligation," thus eliminating any "panic reaction among other business units."[31]. Hence, this approach might also decrease the bankruptcy rate.

Market Stability

Market stability implies a steady and continuous flow of long-term funds to the users through financial intermediaries, such as investment banks or specialized institutions, including industrial and agricultural but not commercial banks. This does not imply, however, that development financing for infrastructure projects will be readily available in an interest-free economy. Odds are that, unless resources in the oil-rich countries are made available by the governments through their respective ministries of finance, local banks would not have sufficient resources to satisfy capital needs in the market. However, there is no reason to believe that this flow of funds would be distorted or minimized after the abolition of interest, if all else remains the same.

Fund Prices

Apart from interest-free loans to home buyers, Islamic long-term financing has a price and it depends on the user's type of financial instrument.[32] In trade related or fixed yield instruments, for example, the price is the margin in murabaha, the rental charges in leasing, and the profit rate in equity finances and PLS schemes in general. It is difficult to predict the trend in these rates or the degree of fluctuation to which they may be subject.

However, the determination of profit rates must follow certain trends. First, these rates are not expected to be fixed or rigid. Second, their determination should not be left, in principle, to the suppliers of funds or the monetary authorities. This does not rule out the need for issuing certain guidelines by the relevant authorities to assist institutions and borrowers in reaching a fair contractual agreement. In the absence of such parameters, determination of the profit rate or rental charges by the landlord and the lessee during the transition would be difficult, with each party wondering what the fair rate is. In the long run, the factors of supply and demand would determine the rate.

In addition, the monetary authorities can indirectly influence the supply of funds by changing the volume of the central bank's deposits with member banks. This would raise or decrease the banks' profit rates, depending on whether a contractionary or expansionary policy is applied, respectively. The rate of profit on these deposits can be regarded as a prime rate in the market. A fluctuation in the prices of stocks is likely to be reduced since trading in options or on margins is expected to be curtailed in an Islamic system. In addition, the speculative demand for money, which is a stabilizing element according to the Keynesian system, would be drastically reduced in an Islamic economic system and there would be no speculation on interest-bearing assets (see the Islamic Demand for Money).[33]

Bach argues that if rising stock prices have been heavily financed by borrowed money, a downturn in the market may precipitate a major collapse in stock prices as lenders calls for cash, and may place serious financial pressure on banks and other lenders. A high market based on credit is thus far more vulnerable than a "cash" market, and is more likely to be a cyclically destabilizing force.

On the other hand, other factors would continue to cause instability in the Islamic system, just as they do in the conventional system. These may include changes in economic policies, fluctuations in exchange rates, and expectations of inflation or deflation. All of these would alter investors' and savers' decisions and expectations.

Economic Activities

Contribution to economic activities is considered one of the key advantages of Islamic banking. Islamic banks' concentration on business activities rather than on home loans is one aspect of this emphasis. Studying the financial plan of the applicant and stressing the profitability of the project helps enterprises grow and prosper. Additionally, the elimination of speculative activities leads to the more efficient allocation of resources than in the conventional system.

The balance between the demand for investments and the supply of financing may be achieved more efficiently than in a system based on passive lending. Generally, the current financial system, with some exceptions, assumes a "permissive" rather than a "promotional" role.[34] In the Islamic system, promotional efforts to attract deposits should be matched with equal efforts to seek profitable enterprises and investors. Failing that, the banking system cannot survive, particularly in the absence of fixed-yield instruments. The ability of the Islamic financial system to finance small businesses that are very active and innovative[35] would further enhance its contribution to economic activities.

Summary

Studying the macroeconomic efficiency of the Islamic financial system, we find the following:

(a) A system of variable rate of return does not necessarily lead to a reduction in the country's aggregate savings/investments. Savers/investors can split their portfolios between risk-bearing and low-risk assets rather than decrease savings and investments.
(b) Equity financing on a PLS basis does not change the level of uncertainty in an enterprise since the outcome of a business is independent of the method of financing.
(c) Uncertainties, or risks, are allocated more equitably than in the conventional system. Banks, savers, and investors can absorb their modest share of loss, if any, without disturbing the entire system through bankruptcies.
(d) Speculation in the stock market is expected to be curtailed as trading in options or on margins is prohibited. This is an indication

of efficiency since the flow of long-term funds can be smoothly channeled through financial institutions to productive enterprises, thus increasing economic activity.

(e) In a PLS or equity market, savers would prefer investments that yield the highest return. Entrepreneurs would try to market projects with the highest profits. In such a market, enterprises might try to keep stock prices as high as possible.

While these conditions may benefit existing shareholders, new savers may shy away since a rising stock price would decrease the price-earnings ratio, which would bring the stock price to its equilibrium level. Probably for this reason, Tobin holds the view that in an interest-free economy the rate of return on capital would be higher than in the conventional system.[36]

Macroeconomic Perspective

Delving further into the macro-level topics discussed above, we review four major subjects, providing examples from Kuwait, which represents a surplus open economy,

1. The balance of payments and the flow of capital.
2. Multipurpose banking.
3. Accessibility to money and the capital market.
4. Deficit financing.

Balance of Payments and Flow of Capital

The Kuwaiti economy has a financial surplus and depends on oil as the main source of its current income. This means that its central bank is unable to exercise control on the monetary base or high-powered money since the Ministry of Finance holds and administers the bulk of the foreign exchange reserves. The balance of payment is affected when the ministry decides to spend locally by calling in foreign reserves.[37] This situation is likely to prevail after the abolition of interest, particularly if the CBK abandons the trend of borrowing from local Kuwaiti banks despite huge government deposits to subsidize conventional banks. This is not to discriminate against Islamic banks, since the CBK is entitled to buy Islamic banks' securities to alleviate their liquidity shortages.

Based on the assumption that investors/savers will not reject the new system, there is no danger of a massive outflow of private capital after the abolition of interest. Nevertheless, the monetary authorities must be able to intervene when necessary to secure the liquidity of the banking system and the stability of the Kuwaiti currency. This brings us to the issue of which tools to use to control the transfer of capital in an interest-free economy.

In the current system, the transfer of capital is normally curtailed through changing the interest rate mechanism and the exchange rate. At present, the exchange rate mechanism seems to be the only method that could be applied in an Islamic open economy. Other measures could be adopted, of course, including a quota on the number of transfers or the amount of each transfer; however, these measures are against the free movement of capital and may not be effective.

The major issue in this context is to establish confidence in the business community. Careful preparation and a nationwide campaign to promote the new system and explain its advantages would eliminate the chances of a massive flight of capital after the abolition of interest.

Multipurpose Banking

Currently, Islamic banks, with the exception of Iranian banks, are permitted to conduct many commercial and non-banking activities. Central among these businesses are (a) the importation of goods for their own account and on behalf of their clients, (b) the development of real estate projects (on March 2011, the Kuwaiti government, upon the CBK's recommendation, allowed Islamic banks to finance mortgage lending on an interest-free basis[38], and (c) the promotion of various types of investments, including commercial and industrial enterprises, through either acquisitions or equity participation.

In an interest-free banking system, the regulators must decide whether or not to allow the banks to enter the market as buyers and sellers of goods and services. The argument in support of permitting Islamic commercial banks to be involved in trade is based on the premise that Islamic banks are not lenders per se and are multipurpose and, as such, should be deregulated. It could also be said that multipurpose banks are more cost efficient in terms of economies of scale and scope.

On the other hand, the augmentation of deposit-taking activities, financing, and general trades leads to the concentration of power in a few hands. This, in turn, leads to monopolies and conflicts of interest and works against the market's specialization of labor. Bank personnel would have access to inside information about their corporate customers, which could be used for illicit gains in share trading. A conflict of interest can arise when a bank's representative sits on the board of a subsidiary or a customer's company, since it is difficult to ascertain whether the officer should look after the bank's interests or the company's.

Accessibility to Money and the Capital Market

The development of an Islamic money market and capital market faces technical and religious reservations. These reservations preclude Islamic banks from tapping the money and the capital market to alleviate their liquidity shortages. There are other objections regarding the transferability of debt obligations, for example, the discounting of commercial bills and selling a bank's debts to a third party. Furthermore, the development of money and capital markets or a secondary Islamic market depends on the marketability, collectability, convertibility, and changes in the market prices of these certificates.

It is difficult to predict at this stage whether an Islamic money market would be efficient or not. Even with the assumption that corporate certificates will be marketable, callable, and convertible, the question of market prices and government regulations remains. The market price of a PLS corporate certificate would be determined by supply and demand, in addition to savers' perceptions of their expected income stream. The volatility of prices will not directly affect yields, as they do in an interest-based system. The yield determinants are exogenous to the price of the certificate, since it is a function of previous trends and the future income of the enterprise issuing the security. Actual or interim results, whether good or bad, will tend to increase or decrease the price of securities, respectively, all else being equal.

The absence of government borrowing and open market operations will tend to restrict the expansion of the Islamic money and capital markets. However, the markets will be enhanced if the government decides to finance public enterprises by selling PLS-denominated securities (see the next section).

The regulations must consider whether or not commercial banks would be prohibited from dealing and underwriting corporate securities. Failure to organize and regularize the market at an early stage will hinder its progress and adversely affect the development of an efficient banking system.

Deficit Financing

In the wake of a persistent budget deficit (present in many Islamic countries) coupled with growth in private sector savings, a proposal for internal borrowing is hereby presented. Now more than ever, Islamic countries require the efficient allocation of resources and the mobilization of private savings. This could be achieved through launching government profit-linked certificates. Profit-linked certificates would be different from ordinary government securities in the conventional system in substance and form. First, it would not be an interest-bearing bond. Second, it would be used for medium- and long-term maturities, with few short-term issues. Third, it must be linked to financing profit-generated projects such as motorway construction (whereby a toll is paid by the users), communications, education, health services, and a host of other projects that meet the following criteria: (a) the cost-benefit relation can be identified and quantified and (b) once the cost-benefit relation is known, by assuming that the benefits outweigh the costs, a portion of the benefits would be distributed annually as yields (to the bearer) until maturity.

I see no reason why the government cannot promote industrial projects by establishing a public shareholding company to manage either one project or a group of projects, since this is common practice in many Gulf countries such as Kuwait and elsewhere.

Industrial enterprises may raise capital or financing from the public on a partnership or mudaraba basis.

Does deficit financing lead to inflation? According to Friedman (1974), that depends on the method of deficit financing[39]:

> If the deficits are financed by creating money they unquestionably do produce inflationary pressures. If they are financed by borrowing from the public, at whatever interest rates are necessary, they may still exert some minor inflationary pressures. Their major effect will be to make Interest rates higher than they would be otherwise.

Based on this argument, it seems that deficit financing on a PLS basis would produce inflationary pressures when money is tight or in poor economies. This does not mean that private wealth in these economies is negligible, nor does it imply that tapping internal markets is futile the objective of tapping the market to finance the budget deficit is to absorb excess liquidity. It may be safely assumed that internal borrowing, if properly timed, would be anti-inflationary. Additionally, the proposed scheme for borrowing from the public would have the plausible effect of avoiding the crowding-out effect. Government spending usually crowds out private spending if not accompanied by taxes or borrowing from the public. This effect is emphasized by Friedman and other econometricians in St. Louis US.[40]

Endnotes

1. For more details see Siddiqi, Issues in Islamic *Banking*, 1983, op, cit., p. 87.
2. Fisher, 1971, p. 269.
3. Bain, op. cit., pp. 242-245
4. The only exception in Bain's view is very large projects, the results of which would affect the welfare of the country as a whole, such as the Channel Tunnel project, op. cit., p. 243
5. Waqar M. Khan op. cit., p. 59.
6. Pringle, 1975, p. 6. See also "Risk Capital, Business Investment and Economic Co-operation," in M. Ali, ed., 1981.
7. Bain, op cit, p.243.
8. Bain, 1981, p. 242.
9. Unless otherwise stated, the analysis in this chapter is concerned with the author's general perception of the situation following the abolition of interest.
10. Ul-Haque and Mirakhor, 1986a, pp. 4-5
11. *From an interview with Dr Anas Zarka, Kuwait 15 December 2013.*
12. Irving Fisher, *the Theory of Interest*, Macmillan, New York, 1930.
13. Kenneth E. Boulding *Economic Analysis, Vol. 1, Macroeconomics*, 4th ed., Harper & Row, 1966, p. 535.
14. Cited in Ul-Haque and Mirakhor, 1986a, p. 4. The same result has been confirmed by Block (1972) and Heinke (1975), p. 5.
15. Waqar M Khan, Towards an Interest-free Islamic Economic System. A Theoretical Analysis of Prohibiting Debt Financing. 1985, pp 36-59.
16. Eamonn Butler, in *Milton Friedman, a Guide to His Economic Thought*, Hants, UK, 1985, pp. 14-17.
17. Cited in Ul-Haque and Mirakhor, 1986a, pp. 4-5. The same results are confirmed by Block (1972) and Heinke (1975) p5.
18. Allocation of Resources op. cit.
19. Boulding, p. 535.
20. "Journal of Comparative Economics", June 1985, pp 208-9
21. A. H. S. Kabbara, "The Final Chapter of the Aftermath of Souk al-Manakh," *Arab Banker Journal*, London: June-July, 1987, pp. 23-24.
22. IMF paper vol 184, pp. 4-8
23. Waqar M Khan, op cit, p 51
24. *See "A* Contribution to the Theory of Consumer Behavior in an Islamic Society" in Khurshid Ahmed, 1980, pp. 9-30.
25. Pryor op. cit. *Also Khurshid Ahmed op, cit.,*

26. *See Khurshid Ahmed op, cit.,*

27. Siddiqi Survey pp 5-6 and Kahf (1992) Waqf.

28. First Zakat Conference, Kuwait, April 30 to May 2, 1984, p. 286.

29. Darweesh A. Fuad and Mahmud S. al-Zein, "The Impact of Zakat on Aggregate Consumption Function in an Islamic Economy," *Journal for Research in Islamic Economics*, Vol. 2, No. 1, 1984, pp. 52-59.

30. Zarqa, ibid, footnote 33, pp 286-294.

31. Zarqa, 1983, pp. 181-188.

32. We are not concerned here with the instrument's pricing mechanism.

33. Quoted in Chapra, 1985, pp. 98-99. See also Zarqa, op. cit., p. 183.

34. Bain, 1981, op. cit., p. 252.

35. A. H. Kabbara, PhD Thesis op., cit.

36. Kartsen, 1983, p. 22.

37. Andrew Crockett and A. Evans, "Demand for Money in the Middle Eastern Countries," IMF papers, Washington D.C: December 1980, p. 553

38. Al-*Seyasseh Newspaper*, March 13, 2011.P. 19.

39. R. J. Gordon, ed., *Milton Friedman's "Monetary Framework*, University of Chicago Press, Chicago, 1974, p. 140.

40. Helmut Frisch, "Monetarist and Monetary Economics, a Delayed Comment," in *the Structure of Monetarism*, Thomas Mayer, ed., W. W. Norton, New York, 1978, p. 120. C. A. Anderson and K. M. Carlson, "A Monetarist Model for Economic Stabilization," *Federal Reserve Bank of St. Louis Review*, April 1970

CHAPTER 15

Conclusion

The relations between Islamic teachings and economics are worthy of note. First, the Quran urges, stresses, and advises mankind in several verses to struggle to reach or to avail of the bounties bestowed by God almighty. For instance, God says, "When the prayer is ended disperse through the earth and seek something of God's bounty" (62:10). Islam also emphasizes the principles of morality and ethics in business transactions by reinforcing the values of justice and fairness. The pillars of economic development are mainly found in a) Islamic norms and values, b) an emphasis on economic growth, and c) justice in the distribution of income and wealth. Adherence to Islamic norms and values is reflected in the Quran, the Sunna and the examples inferred from the behavior of Islamic scholars throughout history.

One might wonder why economic development is related to Islamic norms and values. This is a legitimate question that can be answered by reminding ourselves that man is obliged to seek Allah's protection against poverty, scarcity, and humiliation. The Quran explains that seeking material gains in the pursuit of living by legitimate means is considered *ibadat* (worship). In addition, the Prophet said, "Seeking halal livelihood after fulfilling ones ordained *ibadat* is obligatory."[1] Through zakat, charity, and the inheritance law, wealth, including money, is meant to circulate and change hands. Only through the mechanism of circulation can the economic growth and stability be achieved.

The 1970s witnessed the emergence of Islamic economics with a doctrine that demonstrates the economic features of Islam as applied during the Prophet's time. The prohibition of interest is only a milestone in an economic order generally based on such principles, polices, and practices that were applicable centuries ago. Islamic law, which was applied in a different time frame and social settings, is not fully operational today. Even if we believe, as Muslims, that the Divine Law is applicable anytime, anywhere, there is a wide gap between legal practices and Islamic law. The form and substance of every transaction has no similarity with current practices: for example, the corporation, preference shares, bank ownership versus bank deposits, documentary credit, options, build-operate-transfer contracts, and so forth. Many other examples or laws such as Hisba (the supervision of markets), *Bait al-Mal*, and expropriation in the public interest, are to be adapted to real-world practices. Others, such as the fifth (*al Khums*) and the distribution of Hima'h land are not relevant today as they were centuries ago.

The principal tools of Islamic economics that have positive social implications are the following:

- The zakat levy on income and wealth.
- *Sadaqat, kafarat,* etc.
- The distribution of Hima'h land.
- The allocation of state land for grazing.
- Al-awkaf funds.
- The inheritance law.
- Atonement for vows and oaths.

Private property is well protected and Islamic teachings urge Muslims to develop their wealth without harming others. State or public property is sought to serve society and provide for public utilities and necessities. Neither form of property should impinge on the other; however, public interest comes before private interest.

Justice and equality in Islam imply that people should have equal opportunities but this do not entail their financial equality. The Islamic state is responsible for providing primary necessities to needy citizens. The majority of jurists define the primary necessities as the minimum subsistence level for food, shelter, clothing, medical care, and education, as well as a servant for the disabled.

Islam encourages economic enterprise and investments and morally and institutionally discourages the inability to translate savings into productive investment. It is unlikely that savings will remain dormant, in hoarding, since the imposition of zakat on liquid assets prods savers to turn these into investable funds for fear of being wiped out by zakat.[2] This system tends to increase the supply of investable funds within any given level of aggregate savings. Islamic teachings clearly encourage productive activities and both commercial and philanthropic investments (as in waqf). Nearly eight centuries earlier, Al-Razi (d. 1209 G) explained the reasons for the prohibition of usury in the Quran (2:275), stating that Allah prohibited it because it diverts people away from productive enterprise. A person with money would find it easier to earn a living from extra money through usury than through the hassle of trade and difficult industries that are so essential to society (Vol. 2:352).

The main ingredient of sustained growth is technical progress, which is often commercially risky. Since interest-based finance is not suitable. The availability of venture or equity capital becomes crucial. The following analysis assumes that an Islamic banking system functions along a PLS banking mode. The discussion focuses on the ethical, social and economic benefits the new banking system is likely to achieve.

Categorically, Islamic economics aims at establishing a society based on social justice and the efficient allocation of resources, as well as equal opportunities for all citizens (see Chapter 1). To achieve this in the banking sphere, Islamic economists have reinstated an Islamic financing mechanism based on the PLS principle, as opposed to a guaranteed return, inherent in an interest-based system.

The preceding chapters demonstrate that a PLS system provides a workable and viable alternative to riba. The importance of this finding stems from the fact that the PLS system is no longer an abstract phenomenon. The broader justification for banning riba is to establish a perfect measure for rewarding human effort and capital through the mechanism of PLS. In a PLS system the net positive or negative outcome of an enterprise is shared between human capital and money capital. A positive return adds to the wealth of a society. Thus profit sharing (or a positive return) distributes the creation of wealth in a society more equitably than the rate of interest. The implicit assumption here is that other factors, such as land and labor, are remunerated by rent and just wages, respectively, notwithstanding that labor can share profits too and that a just wage is as equitable as profit sharing.

In an interest-based system, the borrower reaps the fruits of the wealth created or must bear the losses alone. It would be fairer, therefore, if both the lender and borrower shared the additional wealth so created according to an agreed profit sharing ratio. In the event of a loss, it would be unfair for the lender to receive a guaranteed sum while the entrepreneur suffered a loss of return in addition to a decline in assets. Thus, a financial system based on the sharing of profits along with risk or uncertainty lays the ground for establishing social justice and more equitable risk sharing in society.

The cost of funds (to the users) in murabaha and other trade-related instruments would have to be organized and coordinated between the authorities and financial institutions. It is expected that savers and investors would relate the margin (in murabaha or leasing) to interest in the early phases of the abolition of riba. This could be tolerated for a while but eventually the margin would have to reflect criteria that could be laid down after studying the general trend in profit margins in the economy. One of the criteria would be the cash flow generated from a lease-based asset. The rental charges would be a portion of the net cash flow during the rental period.

Government would be encouraged to finance development projects on a PLS basis provided the pertained project(s) earns revenue. Two other methods have been suggested to finance government deficit: through issuing cost-benefit-related securities and through tenders whereby a group of investors sets up a project(s) and leases it back to the government.

In the absence of a discount window and conventional open market operations in an interest-free economy, monetary and policy tools would be limited. The authorities must seek other tools acceptable by Shari'a. Some tools that have been suggested and which seem to offer a powerful mechanism for controlling the money supply function through Islamic open market operations, the central bank's deposits with member banks, and floating PLS bonds. Through these mechanisms the Islamic monetary authority can change the level of money supply and have the desired effect on the financing operations of member banks. Islamic monetary and prudential control would be confined to liquidity and reserve ratios, capital adequacy and self-imposed regulations, and selective control measures. Our analysis rules out changing the banks' rate of profit or depositors' rate of profit to exert monetary control. The depositors' and banks' rates of profit must be determined by the market's supply and demand, in compliance with Islamic law.

As for structural stability, it is expected that the central bank will continue its role, as currently the case, of providing tacit support to the banking sector. If a 100% reserve system were applied, there would be no need for the reserve ratio. Notably, the system would be stapler than a fractional reserve system. For example, altering the reserve ratio by a small fraction would cause a significant change in deposits as a result of the multiplier, leading to instability due to the wide variation between high-powered money and the level of banks' deposits.

Such variation would be eliminated in a 100% reserve system since high-powered money and the money supply would be equated with each other when the multiplier equaled unity. Monetary policy would be curtailed since the monetary authority would not be able to use the reserve ratios to control credit expansion and may have to control the monetary base instead.

In addition, the speculative demand for money, a destabilizing element according to the Keynesian system, would be drastically reduced in an Islamic economic system, since there would be no speculation on interest-bearing assets (see the Islamic Demand for Money).

On the other hand, other factors would continue to cause instability in the Islamic system, just as they do in the conventional system, including changes in **economic policies, fluctuations** in exchange rates, and **expectations** of inflation or **deflation.** All of these would alter **investors' and savers'** decisions and expectations.

Usually inflation is associated with frequent upward adjustment of interest rates to keep pace with rising prices. Firms respond by raising output prices in order to meet a soaring cost of borrowing. The elimination of interest would reduce the effect of cost-push inflation on the level of prices, other things remaining equal. Moreover, an increase in output prices may lead to an increase in the nominal return on saving which means that the real return on savings would be bid up.[3] Consequently, the supply of PLS finance would be enhanced. However, the increase in the level of prices may not always result in a higher net operating margin than before inflation due to price control accompanied by rising factor cost of other inputs.

The demand for PLS capital would be enhanced as entrepreneurs will be able to share the uncertainty of production with the banks. However, if the prospect for profits were certain entrepreneurs would rather prefer to reduce the level of PLS contracts in favour of trade related instruments. By contrast, during recession the entrepreneurs' demand for risk capital is likely to increase as opposed to fixed yield instruments.

In the conventional system a decrease in the nominal value of a bank's asset may oblige depositors to transfer their deposits to other banks. The same could happen in an Islamic bank. However, the capacity of an Islamic bank to absorb external shocks seems to be stronger than a conventional bank if liquidity were under control. Whereas significant erosion in the nominal value of a conventional bank's assets may lead to failure.

An Islamic Bank's investment deposit is used to purchase equity participation and other financial instruments. The depositors' expectations of profits are accompanied by their willingness to take risk. A decline in the bank's assets leads to a devaluation in the nominal value of investment deposits. The depositors can decide to terminate their deposits at maturity and invest the residual (adjusted for capital loss) in another Islamic Bank. Or they may retain their deposits in the expectation of a rebound in the asset value of the bank which might cover their book losses and realize some gain. We can say that a long-term depositor would prefer to retain rather than withdraw this deposit assuming that: (1) investment deposits are long-term in nature, (2) long-terms savers\investors are usually unaffected by cyclical fluctuations in earnings, (3) depositors are not allowed to terminate their deposit before maturity (except in special cases), and (4) a written notice of withdrawal should be given in advance.

Thus it could be said that Islamic Banks can withstand a crisis caused by a decline in their asserts more than interest based banks in the medium term.

For this to occur the demand and supply for loanable funds should be in equilibrium.

Though mudaraba deposits are likely to encounter a loss of return in one year, expected stream of income in the subsequent years might well offset the loss. However, one cannot deny the uncertainty inherent in investment deposits if there were not managed properly. Several investment and financing policies could be applied by an Islamic bank to minimize uncertainties and generate a relatively stable income stream. These policies would include:

- Diversification of mudaraba and investment portfolios among various sectors and groups of investors\entrepreneurs
- Splitting the investor's deposits (with their consent) into:
- Demand deposits which are fully guaranteed by the bank.
- Savings deposits which are not guaranteed but nevertheless, savers may withdraw deposits upon request or whenever they sense any difficulties facing the bank.
- Investment type deposits.

If a bank run occurs, an Islamic bank may become insolvent and may not tolerate withdrawals of neither savings nor demand deposits

There is a call for the creation of innovating approaches to cope with the various needs of financing on the corporate and personal levels. Failing that, corporate borrowers including Islamic banks will find it difficult to obtain short term money to ease liquidity shortages. Likewise, consumers will find it difficult to obtain personal loans, for example for recreational or unspecified purposes. This has advantages and disadvantages. By eliminating financial loans or overdraft, speculations in the stock market will be dwarfed leading to more stable prices. In the absence of lending co-operatives and the limitations of interest free loans disintermediation would be encouraged causing a black market for disguised riba to flourish

Policy makers will face other difficulties concerning behavioral and ethical issues and the necessity to reduce the moral hazard problem (which will hinder the implementation of equity based lending).

Reducing information cost and adapting a PLS system precipitate broadening the professional skills of banks personnel and developing their expertise in project evaluation and Islamic financing methods.

Among the key advantages of Islamic banking are:

- Contribution to economic activities.
- Concentration on business activities rather than on home loans or murabaha.
- Stressing the profitability of the project helps enterprises grow and prosper.
- The elimination of speculative activities leads to the more efficient allocation of resources than in the conventional system.
- Additionally, the balance between the demand for investments and the supply of finance could be achieved more efficiently than in a system based on passive lending.

Currently investors cannot freely switch from one financial institution to another, especially in the case of industrial or home finance. This may be an added advantage since the cost of capital (to the borrower) would be negligible, especially after the abolition of interest. In addition, this condition minimizes the social cost of intermediation should there be a shortage of funds in the private sector. Currently, small commercial firms do not enjoy the same privileges as larger firms in the industry. This, however, has more to do with sectional preferences than shortages of funds.

In the new Islamic system, it would be possible to finance small businessmen who have expertise but lack collateral, irrespective of their social status.

Highlights of the Preceding Chapters

1. Objectives of Islamic economics

Islamic economics encompasses the following objectives:

- The sanctity of private property.
- Banning interest and implementing a banking system based on a partnership between labor and capital through musharaka, mudaraba, and so forth.
- The voluntary introduction of zakat and waqf by banks and investment companies, since one of the main goals of Islamic economics is social assistance, which is a charitable religious contribution.
- Full employment.
- Sustainable economic growth to achieve socioeconomic justice.
- Stability in the value of money due to banning the lending of money for money and the prohibition of regarding money as a commodity.

2. Macroeconomic efficiency

Macroeconomic efficiency is demonstrated in equity financing, risk allocation, and the **banning of speculative activities and** its impact on wealth creation.

- Equity financing on a PLS basis does not change the level of uncertainty in an enterprise since the outcome of a business is independent of the method of financing. However, it relieves the burden of interest from the balance sheet.
- Financial system based on the sharing of profits along with risk or uncertainty lays the ground for establishing financial freedom in society.
- Uncertainties, or risks, are allocated more equitably than in the conventional system.
- Banks, savers, and investors can absorb their modest share of a loss, if any, without disturbing the whole system through bankruptcy. The danger of bankruptcy will be largely reduced in the Islamic system since losses will be borne in proportion to each party's contribution rather than by the borrowers alone.
- Speculation in the stock market is curtailed since trading on options or margins is not allowed. This ban affects positively an interest-free

system and diminishes speculative activities, which are usually enhanced by debt, especially when derivatives and trading on the margin are forbidden.

- The collapse of the U.S. real estate market was the outcome of a bubble created by initial-based lending, as experienced with housing mortgages. These mortgages were wrapped and sold multiple times, creating false demand accentuated by rising prices, which collapsed afterward, in 2008.

3. Wealth creation

- In a PLS or equity market, savers prefer investments that yield the highest return. It is probably for this reason that Tobin holds the view that in an interest-free economy the rate of return on capital would be higher than in a conventional system.
- The flow of long-term funds can be channeled through financial institutions to productive enterprises, thus increasing economic activities.
- In a PLS system the net positive or negative outcome of an enterprise would be shared between human capital and money capital. A positive return adds to the wealth of society.

4. Equitable distribution

- Profit sharing (or a positive return) distributes the creation of wealth in a society more equitably than the rate of interest.
- In an interest-based system the borrower reaps the fruits of the wealth created or must bear losses alone.
- It would be fairer if both the lender and the borrower shared the additional wealth thus created.

5. Economic implications of Zakat

14 centuries ago, the divine law and tradition of the Prophet and his companions introduced the following principles for zakat collection and administration that were innovative then and still are:

- The creation of purchasing power among zakat recipients, thus raising their consumption, if the zakat is distributed in cash.

- The redistribution of wealth and income through the mobilization of idle resources by an amount equivalent to the zakat levy. This may gradually lead to the transfer of wealth from idle owners to more dynamic recipients.
- The encouragement of investments, since it is a tax on accumulated net wealth rather than a tax on income alone. The Prophet addressing his companions said, "Invest the orphans' money so that it may not be wiped out by Zakat."
- The discouragement of hoarding and the establishment of a society based on brotherhood, cooperation, and solidarity, which leads ultimately to the prevention of class wars.
- Subsides for the poor, thus decreasing the burden of the fiscal authorities and freeing government revenue for other productive projects.

Future Research

The elimination of interest is a crucial step in instigating an Islamic economy. There are some controversial issues that remain to be resolved and some hurdles and constraints that should be tackled to pave the way for a smooth transformation, including (i) the effects of an interest-free system on the equilibrating mechanism in the market for loanable funds, (ii) the effect of uncertainty on liquidity preference, hoarding, and the supply of savings among small and low-income bracket savers, (iii) the effects of PLS on the supply of funds to small businesses and risk capital, (iv) ways and means of fostering entrepreneurial activities, (v) the optimal mechanism for profit allocation and distribution among shareholders and depositors/investors in Islamic banks, and (vi) whether depositors/investors in Islamic banks are entitled to share in the profits originating from various services the banks provide?

It would be difficult to install the new system and guarantee its viability without a solid legal framework that regulates instruments and institutions and prescribes the rights and obligations of those concerned. There is a need, however, to establish a legal and technical framework to carry out government borrowing on a PLS basis. More significantly, policy makers must study the implications of PLS borrowing from the public as opposed to taxation in financing government spending vis-à-vis the impact on zakat collection. In addition, I have not seen any studies pertaining to the mechanism for controlling capital outflow in an Islamic economy. Further research in this area is needed. Further research is also needed to devise a framework for the central banks to observe rather than adjust the rate of profit in musharaka or mudaraba financing.

Many fiqh forums have approved the inclusion of interest in the balance sheet of a newly acquired conventional company if the interest-based assets of the acquired company does not exceed 30% of the total assets of an Islamic controlling company.

By applying logic similar to that above, is it permissible to have a dual or mixed waqf, that is fixed property waqf and cash waqf? Further, is it permissible to have cash waqf whereby the cash sum is lent for a fixed yield not exceeding, for example, 5%, provided the cash waqf is no more than 30% of the total benevolent waqf? These questions have been proposed to the same fiqh forums that permitted a ceiling not exceeding 30% interest-based assets in the portfolio of a controlling company.

In conclusion, the path of Islamic economics and finance has a long way to go. Many features and core principles still require further research and investigation. Bridging the gap between sixth-century practices and modern life is a daunting task that requires tacit support to unveil further treasures bestowed in the earliest teachings. Finally, Islamic finance links capital with industry and commerce through PLS arrangements without interest. For the first time in modern history, an Islamic financing mechanism has become a reality. This development is not just a matter of theory anymore but also a dream come true.

Endnotes

1. Imam Malik in *Al Muwatta'*, Vol. 1, p. 251.
2. Ahmad, 'Ziauddin, "Some Misgivings About Islamic Interest Free Banking", Fisal Islamic Bank Lecture Series,, Khartoum, November 1985, p 7.
3. Quoted in Chapra, 1985, pp. 98-99. See also Zarqa, op. cit., 1983, p. 183.

Abbreviations

"AAOIFI"	Auditing and Accounting Organization for Islamic Financial Institutions
"CBK"	Central Bank of Kuwait
"CDs"	Certificate of deposits
"CRIE"	Center for research in Islamic economics
"FRNs"	Floating rate notes
"FRS"	Fixed rate system
"GMS"	Government mudaraba shares
"HCSS"	Higher Committee for Shari'a Supervision
"IB"	Islamic bank
"IBK"	Industrial Bank of Kuwait
"IDB"	Islamic Development Bank
"IFSB"	Islamic Financial Services Board
"IS"	Islamic sukuk
"JKAU"	Journal of King Abdul-Aziz University
"LG"	Letter of guarantee
"PLC"	Profit-linked certificate
"PLS"	Profit and loss sharing
"PTC"	Participation term certificate
"RSB"	Religious supervisory board
"SCB"	Sudanese Central Bank
"SSB"	Shari'a supe rvisory board

Glossary

adam:; nonexistence of an object or a contract

ah'd: obligation, promise, or pledge

al ad'l: justice

aqe

al deen: (religion)

al haj: pilgrimage to Mecca, the fifth pillar of Islam

alinsan: human being

al istishab: convenience

al jalab: those who meet outside the town, driving animals or other commodities for sale

al mal: wealth; money

al-mizan: symbol of justice; lit. Weighing scale

al mulk: sovereign

al nafe's: self or human

al nase'l: offspring or posterity

al-ibar: maxim, lessons from history

al-imarah: development, construction

al-rijal: people, lit. men

amanat: trust or something in custody of a trustworthy person (trustee)

amin: trustee

aq'd: lit. Knot, tie; obligation; in fiqh a legal relationship created by offer and acceptance

arbun: down-payment; a nonrefundable deposit paid by a buyer retaining a right to confirm or cancel

ariya: gratuitous loan of non-consumable property; the gift of usufruct

ay'b: defect; a defect in a commodity that gives the purchaser the right to cancel the sale

ay'n: an existing, tangible thing that is considered unique; a thing, an object as opposed to its usufruct (manfa'a)

batil: void, false, that which is wrongful

bay': sale

bay 'al wafa': sale where the seller has the right to redeem the property by refunding the purchase price

bay'atayn fi bay'a: lit. two sales in one, prohibited by a hadith

bay'mu'ajal: credit sale with payment of the price at a specified later time

bitibi nafs-in: willingly, voluntarily, without reservation

daman: kafelah, guarantee

damin: one who bears daman

darar: damage, harm, loss

dayn: generic property; property defined or contracted for only by its genus, species, and other characteristics (usually fungibles); any property, not an ay'n that a debtor owes

dhimma: lit. compact, bond, obligation, responsibility, protection, security

Ehsan: justice and benevolence

fareyed: duties

fasid: invalid, void, voidable, unsound

faskh: termination, cancellation, rescission

fatwa (pl. fatawa): an authoritative legal opinion issued by a fiqh scholar

fay: distributions of land owned by the state

fiqh: the science of law; the *corpus juris* of classic Islamic law

furu': lit. branches; the derived rules of fiqh

gharar: lit. peril; hazard, risk, or uncertainty

ghasb: usurpation, the invasion of property rights in an open flagrant manner

hadith: saying or act of the Prophet reported by one of his family members or esteemed companions

halal: lawful, licit

hanafi: one of the four Sunni schools of law, founded by Abu Hanifa

hanbali: one of the four Sunni schools of law, founded by Ahmad Ibn Hanbal

haram: unlawful

hawala: contracts of assignment of debt

hiba: gift,

hila: trick

hisba: supervision of markets

hiyal: legal artifices or deception (sign, hila)

huk'm: court judgment; value assigned by fiqh to an act

Ibada: worship

ibadat: acts of worship

ibaha: permissibility, neutrality of moral value; presumption in fiqh that acts are permissible until proof of the contrary is established ibar: drawing lessons

Ihsan: benevolence, kindness, helpfulness

ijab: offer or qabul

ijara: contract of lease and hire; sale or usufruct

ijma: unanimous agreement of all qualified fiqh scholars of an age; one of four roots (usul) of fiqh

Ijtihad: human judgment or jurists' judgments by deduction, jurists' independent reasoning

illa: lit. cause, reason; the basis for an analog (qiyas) between a case as to which the divine law ruling is known and another case the ruling for which is unknown; the characteristic of a case which, when it is found to exist in another cases, justifies applying to those the same fiqh ruling

ina': double sale by which the borrower sell an object to a lender for cash then repurchase it for a higher price on credit, the net result is a loan with interest

inan: to form a partnership in which each partner contributes both capital and work (using the Hanbali definition)

Iqta'h: allocating barren land to the poor for cultivation

iqta'h: lit, grants.

istihsan: habitual preference

istislah: social utility

istisna': a contract between a buyer of products and a manufacturer who undertakes to produce the goods and deliver them later

jahala: ignorance, lack of knowledge; indefiniteness in a contract, often leading to the finding of gharar

ji'ala: reward for a certain act

kafala: contract of guarantee (also called daman)

kamaliyat: luxuries, third category of human needs

kharaj: yield, profit, gain

khiyar al-shart: the right, stipulated by one or both of the parties to a contract, to cancel the contract for any reason for a fixed period of time

khiyar: lit. an option; the power to annul or cancel a contract

ma'ruf: any act, word, or intention commended by Shari'a

maliki: one of the four Sunni schools of law, founded by Malik ibn Anas

manfa'a: use, usufruct

mawsuf fi al-dhimna: something known only by description and owed by a person

mayser: intoxicant game of chance (see the Quran 5:90)

mu'amalat: dealings or transactions among human beings

mudaraba: see qirad

munkar: illegal action, any bad act, word, or intention

murabaha: lit., mark up on sale, an Islamic method for financing trade or the purchase or import of goods

musaqat: an agreement between a land owner and a farmer who undertakes to irrigate and maintain the crops in consideration for a share of the produce.

muzara'a: lit., sharecropping, an agreement between a financier or a land owner and a farmer whereby the former provides land to the latter for cultivation and maintenance

musharaka: partnership or a joint venture between an Islamic bank and a customer or business entity

mutaqawwwam: things whose use is lawful under the Shari'a

nadhr: vow to God

nasi'a: delay in a sale

nisab: threshold; minimum level of income necessary for living

niyya: intention

nusus: text

qabul: acceptance

qada': judgment system or function of the judge

qadi: judge

qanun: law, statute, code

qard: loan of fungible, to be repaid in kind

qard hassan: benevolent loan

qirad (or muqarada): a transaction by which one party provides capital to a second party who manages the fund; terms for a modern bond earning a proportion of the revenues of the projects it finances, with the manager earning another portion

rab al-mal: lit. the owner of the property; a partner who contributes capital

rah'n: pledge, collateral

riba: see al riba

riba: lit. ziyada; an increase over the face value of a loan amount

riba al fadl: riba of excess; an excess in the exchange of ribawi goods within a single genus

riba aljahiliyya: lit. pre-Islamic riba; the riba of pay or increase, referring to a transaction in which a creditor grants an extension in the term of debt in return for an increase in the principal owed

riba al nasia: riba of delay, an exchange of two ribawi counter values, with one due at a later time ribawi: goods or items subjected to fiq'h rules defined by the schools; items sold by weight and by measure, e.g., foods, cerials.

rikaz: minerals and metals

sabab: cause, reason

sadaqa: act of charity

Sahaba: the Prophet's companions

salaf: loan

salam (also called salaf): lit. advance, purchase of item known by specification or description for delivery at a later specified time, with payment of the price in full at the time of fulfillment of the contract

Salat: prayer ordained by God, one of the five pillars of Islam

sarf: currency exchange

Sawm: fasting, the fourth pillar of Islam

Shafi'i: one of the four Sunni schools of law, founded by al-Shafi'i

Shari'a: jurisprudence, the divine law as revealed in the Quran and Sunna

Sharika: partnership, modern company or corporation; applied also to ownership in common

Shart: condition, stipulation

shuritihim: their stipulation

Shurut (pl. of shart): stipulations; genre of legal formula

Sulh: reconciliation or settlement of a dispute

Sunna: habitual practice or behavior of the Prophet during his revelation period

Tahsiniyat: conveniences second kind of human needs or commodities; see daruriyat

Taliq: lit. suspending; conditioning of a contract on an unknown or future event or fact

Taradin or taradi: mutual consent; see the Quran 4:29-30

tasawur: concept

Tawarruq: practice by which a needy person buys something on credit and immediately sells it for cash to a third party in a separate transaction

tawliya: sale at cost

ulama: Shari'a jurists

umran: civilization

Uqud: contracts

Urf: customs or common habit

Ush'r: lit. 10%; agricultural tax on land watered by rainfall

Usul al fiqh: roots of Islamic jurisprudence, sources of Islamic law

Usul al-fiqh: lit. the roots of the fiqh, the sources of law; fiqh legal philosophy and hermeneutics usul: roots, for example, usul al fiqh

wa'd: promise

Wakala: contract of an agency

Wak'f: charitable trust, also trust founded by a person to benefit his heirs

Waqf: form of partnership in which the partners contribute only their creditworthiness, that is, by borrowing capital jointly and transacting with it

Yamin: oath

Zakat: alms tax, the third pillar of Islam

Zakat al Fitr: sadaqat (donations) on the eve of Eid al Fitr

Zulm: injustice, harm caused by ignoring justice

Bibliography and
Selected References

Abdullah S. al Hajri, Valuation of Investment Efficiency of Awkaf Fund in Kuwait, Awkaf General Secretary, Kuwait, 1427 h/2006.

Ahmed N. Kanaan, "Opinions in the Origins of Jurisprudence" (Nazarat fi Elm Osoul al Fiqh), Ministry of Awkaf and Islamic Affairs, Kuwait, 1432 h/2010.

Al -Awadi, R, <u>Distribution Theory in an Islamic Economy,</u> (Arabic) Cairo Al-Azhar 1974.

Abdou, E, Banks Without Interest, (Arabic), Kuwait, Dar Al-E'Tissam, 1389h.

Abu-Asuad, M, Basic Issues in Islamic Economy, International Islamic Union of Student Organisations, The Holy Quran Publishing House, Beirut, 1978.

Abu-Yusuf, al-Qadi, Al-Kharaj, (Arabic), IBK, Kuwait, Dar al-Shurouk, 1985.

Abu-Zahra, M, "The Zakat", 2nd Conference of the Academy of Islamic Research, Al-Azhar, Cairo, 1965.

Abu-Zahra, "Human Society Under the Agis of Islam", 3rd Conference of the Academy of Islamic Research, Al-Azhar, Cairo, 1965.

Abdeen, Adnan N and SHOOK, Dale, N, The Saudi Financial System, Chichester, John Wiley and Sons, 1984.

Abu, Sulaiman, A, "The Theory of Economics of Islam", in Contemporary Aspects of Economics and Social Thinking in Islam, Gary, Indiana, Mulsim Students Association, 1976.

Adam, Ben Yahya, Kitab Al-Kharaj, (Taxation in Islam), A Ben Shemesh, ed, and Trans, Leiden, E I Brill, 1967.

Afar, M A, Nahwa AL Nazarieh El-Igtisadieh Fi'l Islam, International Association of Islamic Banks, Cairo, nd.

Ahmad, Khurshid, ed, Studies in Islamic Economics, Leicester, The Islamic Foundation, 1980.

Ahmad, Khurshid, Economic Development in and Islamic Framework, Leicester, The Islamic Foundation, 1979. Ahmad, Sh, M, Economics of Islam, Lahore, Muhalnad Ashraf Press, 1974.

Ahmad, Sh, M Social Justice in _Islam, Lahore, Institute of Islamic Culture, 1975.

Ahmad, Ziauddin, et al, Fiscal Policy and Resource Allocation in Islam, Jeddah, CRIE & Institute of Policy Studies, 1983.

Ahmad, Ziauddin, Iqbal Munawar and KHAN M Fahim, ads, Money and banking in Islam, Islamabad, Institute of Policy Studies, 1983.

Ahmad, Ziauddin, "Some Misgivings About Islamic Interest Free Banking", FIBS Lecture Series,, Khartoum, November 1985.

Al-Arabi, M A, "Contemporary Banking Transactions and Islam's View Theorem", 2nd Conference of the Academy of Islamic Research, Al-Azhar, 1965.

Al-Arabi, M A, "Investment of Capital in Islam", 2nd Conference of the Academy of Islamic Research, Al-Azhar, 1965.

Al-Arabi, M A, "The Islamic Economy and Contemporary Economy", Proceedings of 3rd Conference of the 4cademy of Islamic Research, Al-Azhar, 1966.

Al-Arabi, M A, "Muhadarat fi Al-Igtisad Al-Islami", Cairo, Al-Sharg Press, 1967.

AL-Awadi, R, Distribution Theory in an Islamic Economy, (Arabic) Cairo, Al -Azhar, 1974.

Al-Finjari, M Sh, Towards an Islamic Economy, Dar OKAZ, Jeddah, 1981.

Al-Amin, Hassan Abdullah, Banks' Cash Deposits and their Investment in Islam, (Arabic), Dar Al-Shurouk, Jeddah, 1983.

Al-Ghazali Abu Hamid Muhammad, Ihya Ulum Al-Din, Kitab Al-shukr Beirut, Dar Al-Marifah, nd.

Al-Hamshari, Mostafa, Al-A'amal Al-Masrafiyyah Fi Al-Islam, Cairo, Majma Al-Buhuth Al.-Islamiyyah, 1973.

Ali, A Al-Salous, Selling, Banking and Money, (Arabic), Dar Al-Haramein, Doha, 1983.

Ali, Maulana Muhammad, ed, A Manual of Hadith, Surrey—UK, Curzon Press, 1977.

Ali, Muazzam, ed, Islamic Banks and Strategies of Economic Co-operation, London, The International Association of Islamic Banks, New Century Publishers, 1982.

Ali, Muazzam, ed, Papers on Islamic Banking, London, New Century Publishers, 1984.

Al-Mawdudi, Abu Al-A'la, Al-Riba, 1st ed, Damascus, Dar Al-Fikr Al-Islami, 1958.

Al-Jarhi M'abid All, "Nahwa Ni.zamiNagdi wa Mali Islami., Al-Haykal wa Al-Tatbiq", Cairo, Al-Itihad Al-Dawli lil Bunuk Al-Islamiyyah, nd.

AL-Jarhi,.M A, "Towards an Islamic Macro Model of Distribution: A Comparative Approach", Journal of Research in Islamic Economics, Vot 11, No 2, (Winter, 1985), Jeddah.

Al-Jarhi, M A, "A Monetary and Fiscal Structure for an Interest-Free Economy: Institutions, Mechanism and Policy", Islamabad Seminar, 1981.

Al-Jawziyyaii, Ibn Al-Qayyim,•A'lam, Al.Mawaqqi'in 'An Rabb Al-Alamin, 1st ed, Vol 1, Cairo, Al-Maktabah Ai-Tijar.iyyah Al-Kubra, nd.

Al-Jassas, Ahkam Al Quran, Cairo, Al-Matba'ah Al-Bahiyyah, Vol 1, 1347h.

Al-jamal, Muhammad Abdul Munim, Mawsu'at Al-Iqtisad AI Islami, Cairo. Dar A.1-Kitab Al-Misri, 1.980.

Al Dusary, T. S., "Precaution (Tahawwut) Contracts", dar Kunuz Ishbelia, Riyad, 2006.

Al -Jarhi M abid Ali, "Nahwa Nizam Naqdi wa Mali Islami, Al-Haykal wa Al-Tatbiq" Cairo Al-Itihad al-Dawli lil Bunuk Al-Islamiyyah, nd.

Al-Jarhi, M, A, "Towards an Islamic Macro Model of Distribution: A Comparative Approach", Journal of Research in Islamic Economics Vol. 11, No2, (winter, 1985), Jeddah.

Al-Jarhi, Mabid Ali, "A Monetary and Financial Structure for an Interest-Free Monetary Economy: Institutions, Mechanism and Policy." Seminar on Monetary and Fiscal Economics, Islamabad, Jan., 1981, in Z. Ahmad, M. Iqbal and M.F. Khan, eds., Money and Banking in Islam, CRIE, Jeddah, and the Institute of Policy Studies, Islamabad, 1983,

Al-Jawziyah, Ibn AL-Qayyim, Alam, Al Mawaqqi in An Rabb Al-Alamin 1st ed, vol 1, Cairo Al-Maktabah Al-Tijariyyah Al-Kubra, nd.

Al-Jassas, Ahkam Al-Quran, Cairo Al-Matba ah Al -Bahiyyah, Vol 1, 1347h.

Al-Jammal, Muhammad Abdul Munim Mawsu at Al -Iqtisad Al-Islami Cairo Dar Al-Kitab Al-Misri, 1980.

Al-Jammal, Garib, Al-Masarif wa Al-Amal Al -Masrafiyyah fi Al-Sharia ah Al-Islamiyyah wa Al-Qanun, Beirut, Dar Al -Shuruq, nd.

Al-Kassasbeh Hamad, A, "The Concept of Islamic Banking and its Role in Economic Development", (Arabic) Central Bank of Jordan, Amman 1982.

Al -Kaaki, Yehya, A The Concepts of Social Order in Islam (Arabic) Dar Al-Nahda Al-Arabia, Beirut, 1981.

Al -Khafif Sh A, "Individual Property and its limits in Islam" Proceedings of the 1st Conference of the Academy of Islamic Research Cairo, Al-Azhar, 1964.

Al Khuwaiter A ben Hamad, *Al Mudaraba fi al-Sharia al Islamieh* dar Kunuz Ishbelieh, Riyad, 2006.

Al -Labban, I, "The Right of the Poor to the Wealth of the Rich" Proceedings of the 1st Conference of the Academy of Islamic Research Cairo, Al-Azhar, 1964.

Al-Mawdudi, Abu Al-A la, Al-Riba, 1st ed, Damascus, Dar Al-Fikr Al-Islam, 1958.

AI, Maulana Muhammad, ed, A Manual of Hadith, Surrey—UK Curzon Press, 1977.

Ali Muazzam, ed, Islamic Banks and Strategies of Economics Co-operation, London The International Association of Islamic Banks, New Century Publishers, 1982.

Ali, Muazzam, ed, Papers on Islamic Banking, London, New Century Publishers, 1984.

Al -Midani Abdulrahman, H. H., Islamic Sharia Higher Committee for Finalizing the Application of Sharia Rules, Kuwait, 1420 h/2000.

Ali M. al Qardawi, "Rules for the Disposition of Debts" (Ahkam al Tassaruf fi al duyun), Islamic World Federation, Mecca, 2002.

Al -Masri, Rafiq, Masraf Al-Tanmiyyah Al-Islami, Beirut Muassast Al-Risalah, 1977.

Al -Masri, Rafiq, "Al-Islam Wa Nuqud" (Islam and Money) CRIE: Jeddah, 1981.

Al -Mousa, A, and Malachlan K, Immigrant Labour in Kuwait, London, Croom Helm, 1985.

Al -Qardawi Yusef, Zakat jurisprudence (Fiqh Al-Zakat), Dar Al-Qalam Beirut, 1981.

Al -Qardawi Yusef, The Law of and the Prohibit in Islam (Al-Halal Wal-Haram Fil Islam), Indianapolis, American Trust Pub, nd.

Special Reference to Major Projects", Paper presented at the Institute Cooperazione Economic Internazionale, Milan, 14 May 1984.

Al -Sadr, Muhammad Baqir Iqtisaduna 2nd ed, Beirut, Dar Al-Fikr, 1968.

Al -Sadr, Muhammad Baqir, Al-Bank Al la Rabawi fi Al-Islam, Beirut Dar AL—Ta awun lil Matbu at, nd.

Al -Sadr, Muhammad Baqir The General Framework of a Bank in Islamic Society Dar Al-Taaruf, Beirut, 1979.

Al -Sarakhsi, Al-Mabsut 1st ed, Vol 22, Cairo Matba at Al-Sa adah, 1324th.

Al -Shatibi, Ibrahim ibn Musa, Al-Muwafiqat Fi Usul Al-Ahkam 4 Vols Cairo Al-Matba ah Al -Salafiyyah, 1933.

Al -Shawkani, Mohammad Ibn Ali, Nayl Al-Awtar Vol 5, Beirut, Dar Al-Jil, 1973.

Al -Sibai, Mustafa, Ishtirakiyyat Al-Islam, Cairo Al-Dar Al -Qawmiyyah, li Tiba ah wa al-Nashr, 1970.

Al -Tabari, Mohammad Ibn Jarir, Tafsir Al-Tabari Cairo, Dar AL-Ma arif 1969.

Al -Tahwi, Ibrahim, Al-Iqtisad Al-Islami Cairo Al-Matabi al Amiriyyah, 2 Vols, 1974.

Al -Tammar, Abdulwahab, "Banking and Financial System in Kuwiat". (Arabic) International Conference on Capital Market Development in Kuwait and Arabian gulf,
Kuwait, 30 April-2 May 1984.

Alvin H. Hansed, Monetary Theory and Fiscal Policy, McGraw Hill, New York, 1949, p. 167.

Ariff, Mohammad, ed, The Monetary and Financial Economics of Islam Jeddah International Center for Research in Islamic Economics 1982.

Arna'ut, Mohammad M, Cash Wakf in Jerusalem during the Ottoman Rule, *Awqaf Journal, Kuwait* No. 9, November 2005. p35

Asad, Mohammad, The Principles of States and Government in Islam, Gibraltar, Dar Al -Andalus Ltd, 1980.

Association of Muslim Social Scientists, "Outlines of Islamic Economics", Proceedings of the First Symposium of the Economics of Islam in North America held in Indianapolis, Indiana, March 1977.

Attia, Jamal, "Industrial Financing Mechanism and the Need for new Mechanism, UNIDO Workshop, Vienna, June 1986.

Auerbach, B, Money Banking and Financial Markets, London, Macmillan press, 1st ed, 1983.

Babilly, Mohammad, M, The Economy and Islamic Sharia, Dar Al-Kitab Al-Lubnani, Beirut 1975.

Badran A Jaber, "Aqd al Istisna'ah fi al Fiqh al Islami beyna Nazarieh wa Tatbik," Industrial
Bank of Kuwait, Kuwait, 2003.

Bain, Andrew, D, The Economics of the Financial System, Oxford, Martin Robertson and Co Ltd, 1981.

Baron, David, P, The Export-Import Bank: An Economic Analysis, New York, Academic Press, 1983.

Bashir, B A, "Banking Without Interest: The Islamic System", <u>Bankers Magazine</u>, October 1982.

Bashir, B A, "Portfolio Management of Islamic Banks" Unpublished PhD Thesis, University of Lancaster, UK, 1982.

Bank Markazi Jomhouri Islami Iran," The law for Usury-Free Banking" Tehran, 1983.

Bell, J R, <u>A History of Economics Thought</u>, New York Ronald Press 1961.

Beit al Mashura, "Technical Issues and Sharia Vision," Ninth International Conference of Islamic Financial Institutions, Kuwait, January 11-12, 2009.

Blackman, Warren, J, <u>The Canadian Financial System</u>, London, Mcgraw Hill, 1980.

Bucaille, Maurice, <u>The Bible The Quran and Science</u>, North American Trust Publications 1979.

Butler Amonn E., in Milton Friedman, a Guide to His Economic Thought, Hants, UK, 1985, pp. 1417.

Cambell, Tim S, <u>Financial Institutions Markets and Economics Activity</u> New York McGraw Hill 1982.

Chapra, M, Umar, "Objectives of Islamic Economics Order", Leicester, <u>the Islamic Foundation</u>, 1979.

Chapra, M, Umar, "The Islamic Welfare State and its Role in the Economy", Leicester <u>the Islamic</u> <u>Foundation</u>, 1979.

Chapra M, Umar, "Monetary Policy in an Islamic Economy" Paper presented at the <u>International Seminar on Monetary and Fiscal Policies of Islam</u>, held in Islamabad, Pakistan, January 1981.

Chapra M, Umar, <u>Towards a just Monetary System</u>, Leicester The Islamic Foundation, 1985 pp 98-9.

Central Bank of Kuwait, "The Kuwaiti Economy in Ten Years", 1980.

Centre for research in Islamic Economics, King Abdulaziz University Jeddeh, <u>Studies in Islamic Economics</u> A selection of papers in Arabic. The First International Conference on Islamic Economics, Mekkah: 21-26 February 1976.

Choudhury, M A, "A Mathematical Formulation of Mudarabah" Proceedings of 3rd National Seminar, <u>Association of Muslim Social Scientists</u>, Gary Indiana 1974.

Choudhury, M A, "Principles of Islamic Economics", <u>Middle Eastern Studies</u> Vol 19, no 1, January 1983.

Council of Islamic Ideology Government of Pakistan "Report on the Elimination of Interest from the Economy", Karachi <u>State Bank of Pakistan</u> Printing Press, 1980.

Crockett, Andrew <u>Money: Theory Policy and Institutions</u>, London Thomas Nelson and Sons Ltd, 1973.

Crockett, Andrew and Evans, "Demand for Money in the Middle Eastern Countries", IMF papers December 1980, p 553

Crosse, H, and HEMPEL, G, <u>Management Policy for Commercial Banks</u>, England Cliffs, Prentice-Hall Inc, 3rd ed, 1983.

Fuad A Darweesh and al Zein Mahmud S, "The Impact of Zakat on Aggregate Consumption Function in an Islamic Economy", Journal of Research in Islamic Economics, No 1, Vol 2 Summer 1982, pp 52-59.

Dennis, Geoffrey E J, <u>Monetary Economics</u> New York, Longmans Inc, 1981.

Doyle, E P, <u>Practice of Banking</u> MacDonald and Evans, 3rd Ed, 1981.

El—Mallakh R, and Atta, J, <u>The Absorptive Capacity of Kuwait</u> Toronto Lexington D,C, Health and Company 1981.

EL-Gousi, A, "Riba Islamic Law and interest", PhD Thesis <u>Temple University</u> USA, 1982.

EL—Ibrahim, H, <u>Al-Kuwait, Derassah Seyassiah</u>, Kuwait, Dar Al-Elm, 1980.

EL—Sheikh, R <u>Economics Growth of the Oil State: Problems and Policies</u>, University of Kuwait, 1973.

El-Najjar A H" <u>Islam and Economics"</u> (Arabic) Aalam Al-Maarefet Kuwait, 1983.

EL-Naggar A, "One Hundred Questions and One Hundred Answers Concerning Islamic Banks", <u>International Association of Islamic Banks</u>, 1980.

EL—Naggar Ahmad, <u>Al-Madkhal ila-Nazarieh al—Iqtisadiah fi al-Manhaj al—Islami</u>, Jeddeh, Dar al—Fikr 2nd Ed, 1974.

Campbell, Tim S, <u>Financial Institutions Markets and Economics Activity</u> New York, McGraw Hill 1982.

Centre for research in Islamic Economics King Abdul-Aziz University Jeddeh <u>Studies in Islamic Economics</u> A selection of papers in Arabic. The First International Conference on Islamic Economics, Makah: 21-26 February 1976.

Dennis, Geoffrey E J, <u>Monetary Economics</u> New York, Longmans Inc, 1981.

De Smogyi J, "Trade in Classical Arabic Literature" <u>Muslim World</u>, 55 (2) April 1965.

Doyle, E P, <u>Practice of Banking</u> MacDonald and Evans, 3rd ed, 1981.

El—Mallakh R, and ATTA, J, <u>The Absorptive Capacity of Kuwait</u> Toronto Lexington D,C, Health and Company 1981.

El-Gousi, A, "Riba Islamic Law and interest", PhD Thesis <u>Temple University</u> USA, 1982.

El-Ibrahim, H, <u>Al-Kuwait, Derassah Seyassiah</u>, Kuwait, Dar Al-Elm, 1980.

El—Shiekh R <u>Economics Growth of the Oil State: Problems and Policies</u>, University of Kuwait, 1973.

Fisher, Douglas, *Money, Banking and Monetary Policy*, Richard D. Irwin, Homewood IL, 1980.

Fisher, Irving, *100% Money*, City Printing Company, New Haven, NJ, 1937.

Fisher, S. N. (ed.), *Social Forces in the Middle East*, Cornell University Press, Ithaca, NY, 1955.

Friedman, Milton, *the Control of Money, Capitalism and Freedom*, Chicago University Press, Chicago, 1962.

Friedman, Milton, *The Control of Money: A Program for Monetary Stability*, Fordham University Press, New York, 1957.

Garcia, F. L., *How to Analyze a Bank Statement*, 6th Ed., Bankers' Publishing Company, Boston 1979.

Green, Terry, and Webster, John, *Managing Mathematically*, Macmillan Press London, 1976.

Gordon R. J., ed., *Milton Friedman's "Monetary Framework*, University of Chicago Press, Chicago, 1974, p. 140.

Hamdi, Abdulrahim, "The Operations of Faisal Islamic Bank, Sudan", Faisal Islamic Bank Sudan, 1981.

Henderson, J., and R. E. Quandt, *Microeconomic Theory*, McGraw—Hill, London, 1958.

Homoud, Sami, Evolution of Banking Operation in Compliance with Sharia, 2nd ed. Amman, Dar Al Fikr, 1982.

Horvitz, Paul M., and Richard A. Ward, *"Monetary Policy and the Financial System"*, 5th ed., Prentice-Hall, Englewood Cliffs, NJ, 1983.

Hosek, William, *Monetary Theory*, Richard Irwin, Homewood, IL, 1975.

Ibn Abdin Mohammad, Radd Al Muhtar ala Al -Durr Al-Mukhtar, Cairo, Dar al-Sa'adah, 1324 h.

Ibn Hazem, "Al Muhalla", al Matba'h al Muniriyah, Cairo, 1947.

Ibn Khaldoun, *Abdul-Rahman, "Al Muqaddimah"* al Kitab al'Lubnani, Beirut, 1979.

Ibn Qudamah, Al *Mughni*, Vol. 4, 3rd ed., Dar Al Manar, Cairo, 1367 h.

Ibn Taymiyyah, "Taqi al Din Ahmad," *Al Fatawa*, Vol. 31, Matba'at al Riyadh, Riyadh, 1383 h.

International Bank for Reconstruction and Development, *The Economic Development of Kuwait*, John Hopkins Press, Baltimore, MD, 1964.

International Conference of Islamic Economics "Insuring against Risk in Islamic ShariaSixth Round, Kuwait, April 1920, 2011.

International Conference of Islamic Financial Institutions, "The Repercussions of the International Financial Crisis," dar al Raqabeh, Kuwait, 1429 h/2008.

Islamic Counsel of Europe, *The Muslim World and the Future Economic Order*, Islamic Information Service, London, 1979.

Islamic Development Bank, Annual Reports, Jeddah.

Iwai, Satoshi, "A New Approach to Human Economics: A Case Study of an Islamic Economy" working paper, International University of Japan.

Jacobs, Donald P. et al. *Financial institutions*, 5th ed., Richard D. Irwin, Homewood, IL, 1972.

Johnson, H. G., *Selected Essays in Monetary Economics*, George Allen and Unwin, London, 1978.

Johnson, I., and W. Roberts, *Money and Banking*, 2nd ed., Dryden Press, New York, 1985.

Kabbara, A.S., "Islamic Banking: A Case study of Kuwait" unpublished doctoral dissertation, Loughborough university of technology, Loughborough, 1988, p. 338.

Kabbara, A. H. S., "Islamic Finance, A Divine Instrument for African prosperity", Johannesburg-South Africa, October 2007.

Kabbara, A. H. S., "Islamic Banking in Lebanon, Financing Types and Tools," al Nahar daily Beirut, 2-3 September 1998

Kabbara, A. H. S., "Industrial Financing Activities of Islamic Banks," United Nations Industrial Development Organization. Proceedings of a Workshop on industrial Financing by Islamic Banks, Vienna, June 16-20, 1986.

Kabbara, A. H. S., "The Islamic State and Economic Intervention," *Arab Banker*, Vol. 6, No. 6, 1986, Pp 26-28

Kabbara, A. H. S., "The Debt Crisis in Kuwait," *Arab Banker*, Vol. 6, No. 2, 1986 pp 15-17.

Kahf, M., "Fiscal and Monetary Policy in an Islamic Economy: A Theoretical Analysis of a Three Sector Model," presented at the International Seminar on Monetary and Fiscal Economics of Islam, Mecca, 1978.

Kahf, Munzer, "A Contribution to the Theory of Consumer Behavior," in Khurshi d Ahmed (Ed) Studies in Islamic Economics, The Islamic Foundation: Leicester, UK 1980 pp 9-30.

Kahf, Munzer, "Qirad Bonds and their Application", JKAU-Islamic Economics, Vol.7, No.1, 1995 pp 51-73.

Kahf Munzer, "Medium and Short-Term Investment Bond," paper presented at the Fifth Islamic Fiqh Meeting, Kuwait Finance House, Kuwait 2-4 November 1998.

Kassem, Omar, "The Monetary Sector of the Kuwait Economy," Development Seminar Paper, No. 43, School of Oriental and African Studies, February 1984.

Keynes, John, M., *the General Theory of Employment, Interest and Money*, Harcourt, Brace and World, New York, 1936.

Khan, Fahim M., "Islamic Financial Institutions," Ed., Islamic Research and Training Institute, IDB Jeddah 1995.

Khan, Mohsin, S., and Abbas Mirakhor, "The Financial System and Monetary Policy in an Islamic Economy," DM/85/72, International Monetary Fund, Washington, DC, November 1985.

Khan, Mohsin S., "Islamic Interest-Free Banking: A Theoretical Analysis," *International Monetary Fund Staff Papers*, Vol. 33, No. 1, March 1986.

Khan, Shahrukh Rafi, "Profit and Loss Sharing: An Economic Analysis of an Islamic Financial System," doctoral dissertation, University of Michigan, 1983.

"Al Iqtissad al Islami" Al Markaz al'alami Li Abhath al Iqtisad al Islami, King Abdulaziz University Press, Jeddah, 1980.

Kuwait Awkaf Public Foundation, Issue No. 11, Year 6, Zu alqe'deh 1427, November 2006.

Kuwait Awkaf Public Foundation, Issue No. 7, Year 4, Shawal 1425, November 2004.

Kuwait Chamber of Trade and Industry, Memorandum of Reactivating the Kuwait Economy, Kuwait, February 1984.

Lipsey, Richard G., *An Introduction to Positive Economics*, 6th ed., Widenfield and Nicholson, London, 1983.

Llewellyn, David T., "Evolution of the British Financial System," Loughborough University of Technology, *Research Paper Series,* No. 1, February 1985.

Machneih, M. J., *Islam in a Modern Perspective* (in Arabic), Dar al—Elm L'Lmalayeen, Beirut, 1981.

Makinen, Gail E., *Money, the Price Level and Interest Rates*, Prentice-Hall, Englewood Cliffs, NJ, 1977.

Malik, Imam, *Al-Muwatta*, Diwan Press, Cambridge, 1982.

Ministry of Awqaf and Islamic Affairs, *Mudaraba, Company: A Preparatory Edition of Samples of Thesis for Islamic Law Encyclopaedia*, Dar Al Siyasah Press, Kuwait, n.d.

Ministry of Awqaf and Islamic Affairs, "A Preparatory Edition of Samples of Thesis for Islamic law Encyclopedia: Companies," Dar Al Siyasah Mohammad S al Haddad, "Current Kuwait Society and the Circumstances of Finalizing the Application of Sharia Rules," Higher Committee for Finalizing the Application of Islamic Sharia, Kuwait.

Mohammad Kamal Hassan, *Application Features in Civilized Islamic Doctrine*, A. Barghut and Y. Sawalhi (trans.), Ministry of Awkaf and Islamic Affairs, Kuwait, 2008.

Mohammad S. al Haddad, "Current Kuwait Society and the Circumstances of Finalizing the Application of Sharia Rules," Higher Committee for Finalizing the Application of Islamic Sharia, Kuwait.

Mohsen, Mohamad, "Assessment of Corporate Securities in Terms of Islamic Investment Requirements," Center for Research in Islamic Economics, 1982.

Moosa, I. A., "Liquidity Functions in the Kuwait Economy," *Industrial Bank of Kuwait Papers*, No. 9, June 1983.

Moosa, I. A., "A Study of the Kuwait Monetary Sector," doctoral dissertation, University of Sheffield, 1986.

Muaz, Abdulmajid B., "al Awkaf wa al Muhtaseb", Awkaf journal No 2, Kuwait May 2002, pp.48-54

Muslehddin, Muhamad, *A'mal, al Bunuk wa al sharia al Islamiyyah*, al Sharikah al Muttahidah Lil Tawzi, Beirut, 1976.

Muslim, A. G., "The Theory of Interest in Islamic Law and the Effects of Interpretation of This by the Hanafi School up to the End of the Mughal Empire, doctoral dissertation, University of Glasgow, 1974.

Naqvi, S. N. H., "Interest Rate and Inter-Temporal Allocative Efficiency in an Islamic Economy," presented at International Seminar on Monetary and Fiscal Economics of Islam, Mecca, 1981. pp. 115-116

Naqvi, Sayed N. H., *Ethics and Economics: An Islamic Synthesis*, the Islamic Foundation, Leicester, UK 1981.

Nevitt, P. K.," Project Financing", London, Euro Money Pub. Ltd., 1979.

Nienhaus, Volker, "Islamic Banking: Microeconomic Instruments, and Macroeconomic Implications," *Arab Banker*, Vol. 6, No. 6, 1986.P 5.

Occasional Papers in Economics, J. Revel (ed.), No. 14, University of Wales Press, 1978.

Ojail al Neshami, "Al Riba, a Disease in the International Economy," Third International Islamic Conference, Kuwait, 2008.

Presley, John R., A *Guide to the Saudi Arabian Economy*, Macmillan, London, 1984.

Pringle, R., *Banking in Britain*Methuen, London, 1975.

Pryor, Fredric L., "Islamic Economic System," *Journal of Comparative Economics*, Vol. 9, No. 2, June 1985.

Qureshi, Anwar Iqbal, *Islam and the Theory of Interest*, Ashraf Press, Lahore, 1974.

Qutb, Sayed, *Interpretation of Ayat Al-Riba*, Dar al-Shurouk, Cairo, 1980.

Qutb, Sayed, *Social justice in Islam*, John D. Hardie (trans.), American Council of Learned Societies, New York, 1970.

Qutb, Sayed, *This Religion of Islam*, 6th ed., International Islamic Federation of Students Association, Polygraphic Press, Malaysia, 1982.

Rahman, Afzalur, *Banking and Insurance*, Muslim Schools Trust, London, 1979.

Revel, Jack, *Solvency and Regulation of Bank: Theoretical and Practical Implications*, University of Wales Press, Wales 1975.

Rida, Mohammad Rashid, *Tafsir al Manar*, 4th ed., Maktabat al Qahira, Cairo, 1960.

Rodinson, Maxime, *Islam and Capitalism*, Penguin Books, London, 1974.

Rosenthal, E. I. J., *Political Thought in Medieval Islam*, Cambridge University Press, Cambridge, 1962.

Rosenthal, Franz (trans.), *an Introduction to History, by Ibn Khaldoun*, 2nd ed., Rutledge and Kegan Paul, London, 1967.

Sami al Suwaylim, 'Precaution (al Tahawwut) in Islamic Finance", Islamic Development Bank, Jeddah, 1428 h.

Sami H. Homoud, "Development through Islamic Financing Instruments," Fifth Islamic Fiqh Meeting, Kuwait Finance House, Kuwait, 1998.

Samuelson, Paul A., *Economics*, 10th ed., McGraw-Hill, New York, 1976.

Schacht, Joseph, *An Introduction to Islam ic Law*, Oxford University Press, London, 1964.

Shalabi, Farouk, "Central Bank's Bills," International Conference on Capital Market Development in Kuwait and the Arabian Gulf, Kuwait, April 3 to May 2, 1984.

Siddiqi, M. N., *"Central Banking in an Islamic Framework"*, Center for Research in Islamic Economics, Jeddah, 1986 p 31.

Siddiqi, M. N., *Economic Enterprise in Islam*, Islamic Book Center, London, 1979.

Siddiqi, Mohammad N., *Muslim Economic Thinking*, Islamic Foundation, Leicester, 1981.

Siddiqi, Mohammad, N., *Issues in Islamic Banking*, Islamic Foundation, Leicester, 1983.

Simon, Henry, *A Positive Program for Laissez Faire: Personal for Liberal Economic Policy*, University of Chicago Press, Chicago, 1948.

Simpson, Thomas, *Money, Banking and Economic Analysis*, Prentice-Hall, Englewood Cliffs, NJ, 1976.

Smogy D. J, "Trade in Classical Arabic Literature" <u>Muslim World</u>, 55 (2) April 1965.

State Bank of Pakistan, various circulars and regulations.

Thomas, Lloyd B., *Money, Banking and Economic Activity*, Prentice-Hall, Englewood

Udovitch, A. L., *Partnership and Profit in Medieval Islam*, Princeton University Press, Princeton, 1970.

Udovitch, A. L. (ed.), *The Islamic Middle East (700-1900): Studies in Economics and Social History*, Darwin Press, Princeton, 1981.

Ul-Haque, Nadeem, and Abbas Mirakhor, "Optimal Profit-Sharing Contracts and Investments in an Interest-Free Islamic Economy," World Bank and the International Monetary Fund, Washington, DC, March, 1986a pp 28-30.

Ul-Haque, Nadeem, and Abbas Mirakhor, "Saving Behavior in an Economy Without Fixed Interest," Discussion Paper No. DRD 184, World Bank, Washington, DC, August, 1986b.

Wafi, A. A, "Economic Integration in Islam," Proceedings of the Sixth Conference of the Academy of Islamic Research, Al-Azhar, Cairo: 1971 PP 768-769

Wafi, A. A., *"Equality in Islam"*, Maktabat, Jeddah, 1983.

Wahid, Abu N. M., *Islamic Banks and a Theory of Optimal Profit Sharing*, Islamic Research Institute, Islamabad, n.d.

Waqar M Khan, Towards an Interest-free Islamic Economic System. A Theoretical Analysis of Prohibiting Debt Financing. In Khan M and Mirakhor A. Eds. Theoretical Studies in Islamic banks and Finance. Housten 1985, pp 36-57.

Wehr, Hans, *A Dictionary of Modern Written Arabic*, J. M. Cowan (ed.), Librairie du Liban, Beirut, 1960.

Wilson, Rodney J. A., *Banking and Finance in the Arab Middle East*, Macmillan, Surrey, 1983.

Wohlers-Scharf, T., *Arab and Islamic Banking: New Business Partners for Developing Countries,* Centre, Paris, 1983.

Yusef, Ibrahim Yusef, *Economic Development Strategy and Technique* (in Arabic), International Association of Islamic Banks, Cairo, 1981.

Zarqa, Anas, "Capital, Allocation, Efficiency and Growth in an Interest—Free Islamic Economy," *Journal of Economics and Administration*, No. 16, November, November 1982, pp.43-58

Zarqa, Anas, "Islamic Economics: An Approach to Human Welfare," in *Studies in Islamic Economics*, A Khan (ed.), Islamic Foundation, Leicester, 1980, pp3-18

Zarqa, Anas, "Stability in an Interest—Free Islamic Economy, A Note," *Pakistan Journal of Applied Economics*, winter 1983. Vol 11, No 2, pp 181-188.

Zarqa, Mustafa, A., "Al-Masaref Muamalatuha, Wadaeha, and Fawaeduha," [Banks' Transactions, Deposits and Benefits], discussion paper, Center for Research in Islamic Economics, *Series*, No. 13, 1983.